This fascinating guide book celebrates w.
unique multi-cultural city. The author's i
times to last week's newest restaurant ope
thusiasm and encyclopedic knowledge of his subject have made Joel Stein a
virtual local legend. For visitors as well as residents, *Santa Fe in a Week* is a
must read for planning an unforgettable evening, weekend or weeklong visit
to the City Different.

John Hatch
2009 Winner of the Sargent Shriver Award for
Distinguished Humanitarian Service

Regardless of whether you are a newbie or a Santa Fe know-it-all, *Sana Fe in
a Week (more or less)* is absolutely indispensible. You will get to where you
are going with it even if you didnt know that was where you were going! It
provides so many suggestions and choices to the many places and experi-
ences that Santa Fe has to offer. Full of insider and practical information,
it needs to be on the bedside table of every traveler no matter when they
arrived. The City Different now has a guidebook showing just how unique
and bounteous it truly is.

Christine Mather
Author of *Santa Fe Style* and *Santa Fe Homes*
New Mexico museum curator

I love this book. It is so helpful and chock full of information.The writing
is clear and the photos are really nice and also helpful. This book will make
my next trip to Santa Fe more enjoyable and easy to plan.

Joyce Trifilleti
San Diego, California

Joel Stein is a phenomenal guide and everyone had very favorable comments.

Cindy Kellett
Akron Art Museum
Akron, Ohio

I am impressed by Joel Stein's profound insights in history and his apprecia-
tion of spirituality.

George A. Adriaenssens
Atlanta, Georgia

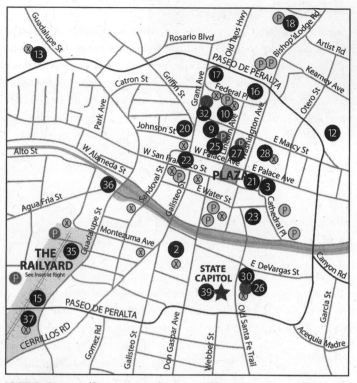

① Bataan Museum
② Bataan Memorial
③ Cathedral Basilica of St. Francis of Assisi
④ Center for Contemporary Arts
⑤ Chamber of Commerce/Santa Fe Outlets
⑥ Children's Museum
⑦ Christo Rey Church
⑧ Christus St. Vincent's Hospital
⑨ City Bus Station
⑩ City Hall
⑪ Santa Fe University of Art and Design
⑫ Cross of the Martyrs
⑬ De Vargas Center Mall
⑭ Dog Park
⑮ Farmers Market
⑯ Federal Courthouse
⑰ Federal Post Office
⑱ Fort Marcy Complex
⑲ Genoveva Chavez Community Center
⑳ Georgia O'Keeffe Museum
㉑ Museum of Contemporary Native Arts
㉒ Lensic Performing Arts Center
㉓ Loretto Chapel
㉔ Museum Hill - Indian Arts & Culture, Folk Art, Spanish Colonial Art, Wheelwright Museum
㉕ New Mexico Museum of Art
㉖ New Mexico Department of Tourism
㉗ Palace of the Governors/New Mexico History Museum
㉘ Public Library
㉙ Rodeo Grounds
㉚ San Miguel Mission
㉛ Santa Fe Community College
㉜ Santa Fe Community Convention Center
㉝ Santa Fe Country Club
㉞ Santa Fe Place Mall
㉟ Santa Fe Southern Railway/New Mexico RailRunner
㊱ Santuario de Guadalupe
㊲ SITE Santa Fe
㊳ St. John's College
㊴ State Capitol

SANTA FE
in a Week
(more or less)

by Joel B. Stein

Photographs by
Alan Pearlman

Historic sites, restaurants, lodging,
shopping, countryside tours

A guidebook designed for the short stay with
recommendations selected for their variety and
historical significance

CHAMISA PRESS

Santa Fe, New Mexico

Published by: Chamisa Press
                  717 Juniper Drive
                  Santa Fe, NM 87501

ISBN 978-0-615-4938-4

Second Edition

10 09 08 07 06 05 04 03 02

Cover photograph: Institute of Archeology, Museum Hill © 2011 Alan Pearlman
All photographs © 2011 Alan Pearlman, except as otherwise noted
Frontispiece map © *The Santa Fean*, used with permission
Cover design by Andrew Neighbour, MediaNeighbours.com
Interior design and typography by Mary Neighbour

Printed in Canada

For Rowan, Anna, Haley, Mason, Jack, Vivian and Raymond

Contents

144
TAOS

158
THE PUEBLOS

183
LA TRIVIATA

APPENDIX
(A SURVIVORS' GUIDE)

207
INDEX

PREFACE

Bienvenido! Welcome to Santa Fe—the "City of Holy Faith." Whatever enticed you to come here, whoever told you of the wonderment you may experience here, we are delighted that you've arrived. Since the publication of the first edition, changes have been taking place in our city. New shops, restaurants and spas have opened. A new addition to the Palace of the Governors, the History Museum of New Mexico, opened on Memorial Day Weekend of 2009; the Railyard Project consisting of art galleries, restaurants, movie theatres, gardens, bikeways, a Farmer's Market and teen center, bring a renaissance to the Railyard and Guadalupe Street. The new Santa Fe Community Convention Center on Marcy Street was opened in September 2008. But remember, the more things change, the more they remain the same. This is so true of historic Santa Fe.

I've been a docent at the Palace of the Governors for many years, as well as a professional guide, and during that time, I have had the pleasure of connecting with people from all over the world. Most of these travelers say that they're visiting Santa Fe for less than a week, and many have come for only a day or so. Yet these visitors find themselves toting substantial stacks of guidebooks—formidable tomes dispensing far more information than the average person could possibly digest in such a brief time.

Taking a cue from you, our very welcome tourist, this book has been designed for the traveler who visits for a few days, a week or perhaps a touch more. We haven't noted every last thing there is to do or see in this magnificent, centuries-old city. That would be impossible and, in any event, contrary to our mission, which is to share with you several days worth of local Southwestern magic, history and highlights. Listed in the book are relevant, related websites, sites that will assist you in planning your trip and in making reservations.

To experience all of Santa Fe, you must come back and visit often! Or, perhaps you will decide to move here, as I did. Now, I'm happily immersed in this city of three cultures, living each day with history at every turn, charm on every city block—museums, music, theater, opera, hiking, skiing and, of course, fabulous dining. Who could ask for anything more?

Perhaps D. H. Lawrence said it best: "I think New Mexico was the greatest experience from the outside world that I have ever had. It certainly changed me forever. . . . The moment I saw the brilliant, proud morning sunshine high over the deserts of Santa Fe, something stood still in my soul, and I started to attend. . . . In the magnificent fierce morning of New Mexico one sprang awake, a new part of the soul woke up suddenly, and the world gave way to the new."

—Joel B. Stein
Santa Fe, 2011

I'm in Love with Santa Fe

I'm in love with Santa Fe;
Like it better everyday;
But I wonder, every minute
How the folks who aren't in it
Ever stand it, any way,
Not to be in Santa Fe.

by Mae Peregine
Santa Fe, 1915

Note: The information in this guidebook was confirmed at press time. We recommend, however, that you call your destinations before traveling to obtain the latest information.

SANTA FE
A SHORT HISTORICAL OVERVIEW

In 2010, Santa Fe officially celebrated the 400th anniversary of its founding by the Spanish in 1610. That date, however, is just an estimate. While the Spanish were probably in Santa Fe as early as 1606-07, actual building of the city did not commence until a few years later.

In 1598, Juan de Oñate led a group of settlers north from Mexico to carve out a settlement, stopping in the area of Ohkay Owingeh (San Juan Pueblo). This settlement did not last, as the group was disappointed in not finding any gold. Shortly afterwards, the new governor Pedro de Peralta was sent to New Mexico to found a permanent settlement. The result was *La Villa de Santa Fe*—the City of Holy Faith. In 1609-10, a decade before settlers landed at Plymouth Rock, the Spanish settlers laid out their new plaza and began building a fortress, the Palace of the Governors, the oldest continuously occupied public building in the country, which is now part of the History Museum of New Mexico.

Early Indian Influences

In the 1880s Adolph Bandelier (Bandelier National Monument is named for him) speculated that two distinct sites in modern Santa Fe were built over pueblos. One was by Ft. Marcy (near the current Cross of the Martyrs) and the other near San Miguel Mission Church on Old Santa Fe Trail, now considered the oldest church in the United States, built around 1610. Edgar Lee Hewett, a renowned archaeologist, believed that the Palace of the Governors was a site of another pueblo. In fact, historical and archaeological studies now indicate that it was the first building on that site.

New Mexico has been populated since prehistoric times. During the Paleo-Indian Period (9500-5500 BCE*), the ancient peoples were hunters and gatherers who wandered across grassy plains searching for food (the climate was different then). The Archaic Period (5500 BCE-600 CE*) followed; during this time people invented new tools and wandered less. They began cultivating corn, beans and squash. Enough moisture was still available that they did not need to be near the river to grow food. By the end of this period, people were settling into villages, building pithouses and starting to make and use pottery.

Most of the ruins you can visit today date from the Ancestral Pueblo Period (400-600 CE-1425 CE). During the early part of this period, people adopted a still more settled lifestyle and began to build larger pithouses. The pottery they used for food storage was now more refined and decorated. Gradually, they began to build dwellings above ground and likely used pithouses more for ceremonial purposes. By the 1300s, some built large, multi-storied pueblos in areas rich with wild plants and game animals. Lack of rainfall may have sent them to areas far from Santa Fe. Many settled in the area of the Four Corners (including Mesa Verde and Chaco Canyon), where the peak population was estimated at between 25,000 and 50,000. Drought is a common occurrence in the Southwest. (Between January and July of 2006, the city had the least amount of rainfall for that period in 112 years.)

The site of the city of Santa Fe was originally occupied by a number of Pueblo Indian villages with founding dates approximately between 400-600 CE to 1300 CE. In 2007-08 as the new Santa Fe Community Convention Center was being built, excavations turned up hundreds of artifacts, including human remains. Other early pueblos in and around the Santa Fe area included Arroyo Hondo, Agua Fría, San Cristobal and Pindi. Many smaller sites dot the landscape around Santa Fe, and you may accidentally come across one while hiking. If so, please leave any artifacts where you find them.

Most archaeologists agree that these sites were abandoned about 200 years before the Spanish arrived and little evidence of them remains in Santa Fe today.

*   BCE denotes Before Christian Era, CE denotes Christian Era.

This period saw the beginnings of what became the present-day pueblos of Taos, Picuris, Ohkay Owingeh, Santa Clara, Kewa (Santo Domingo), San Ildefonso, Jemez, Tesuque, Nambé and Pojoaque. Pecos Pueblo, later abandoned, was also inhabited at that time.

Period of Exploration and Early Spanish Settlement (1540-1680)

In the summer of 1540, an expedition from Spain led by Francisco Vásquez de Coronado reached the area just west of Albuquerque. In spite of initial good relations, tensions soon developed, and many Pueblo people were killed before the Spanish left to explore the southern Great Plains. The following years saw various incursions of Spanish soldiers and priests, often with violent results. During these years, however, the Pueblo populations were reduced more dramatically by European diseases such as smallpox, measles and influenza than they were by battle.

In 1598, Juan de Oñate led a large contingent of soldiers, farmers and priests up to Neuva España (New Mexico) to begin a permanent settlement. He selected land near the Rio Grande at Ohkay Owingeh (San Juan Pueblo), 25 miles north of what is now Santa Fe. The next governor-general, Don Pedro de Peralta, founded *La Villa Real de Santa Fe* (The Royal City of the Holy Faith) in late 1609 or early 1610.

Most of the city was laid out and built between 1610-1612. As previously mentioned, the Casa Real, now called the Palace of the Governors, was originally built as a fortress. It had two lookout towers and its windows were gun slits. It is considered the oldest public building in continuous use in the United States and currently houses the History Museum of New Mexico. An addition was built and opened in the spring of 2009.

The city grew and life was without major incident. Spanish missions, farms and ranches were established. The *Camino Real* (Royal Road) was opened, following the Rio Grande River to Mexico.

For the next 70 years or so, Spanish soldiers and officials, as well as Franciscan missionaries, sought to subjugate and convert the Pueblo Indians of the region, who became essentially enslaved. Their religious, political and socials customs were undermined; in fact, their religious practices were considered witchcraft by the Spanish. Their *kivas* (underground ceremonial chambers) were constantly being filled up with dirt, an action that denied them access to their religious practices. Failure to adhere to Spanish bidding resulted in harsh punishment.

Growing resentment led to skirmishes with bloodshed on both sides, including burning and destruction of entire pueblos, that culminated in the Pueblo Revolt of 1680. On August 10, 1680, warriors from several pueblos in the Santa Fe area attacked the city. This uprising was led by a medicine man known as Po'pay from Ohkay Owingeh, who acted in response to a message from three spirit figures in a *kiva* at Taos Pueblo. The Pueblos communicated with each other by means of runners carrying a cord of maguey fiber with knots tied in it to indicate the number of days to wait for rebellion. When all the knots were untied, the Indians began their attack. By August 21, the Spanish had abandoned Santa Fe. Twenty-one clergymen and 380 soldiers and settlers had been killed. The remaining settlers and troops retreated to what is now El Paso, Texas, where they remained for twelve years. This stands as the only successful Indian uprising in the history of North America. This was a blow to Spanish Colonial control in New Mexico, but it was not the end of Spanish dominance.

Later Spanish-Colonial Period (1692-1821)

Pueblo Indians occupied Santa Fe until 1692, when Don Diego de Vargas reconquered the region and entered the capital city after a "bloodless" siege. On September 13, 1692. de Vargas led his troops into Santa Fe. Using diplomacy, he managed to negotiate a truce with the Indians. De Vargas, a trained soldier with twenty years of experience, was the proper man for the assignment. But it was one he did not want. He loathed this part of the world, really hungering for a post in the Philippines or Havana. In the words of John L. Kessell in *Santa Fe–History of an Ancient City*, DeVargas aspired to improve his post, to escape what he termed the *zozobra*, the wrenching anguish, brought on by "the adversities and perils of that government of New Mexico." In 1926, artist Will Shuster took that word *zozobra* and transformed it into a three-foot puppet that he named Zozobra, or "Old Man Gloom," which he burned at a private Santa Fe Fiesta party to the delight of his friends. The burning of a much-larger Zozobra (in 2008 it was over 49 feet) became a tradition to destroy the gloom at the start of the Fiesta every September.

De Vargas was imprisoned in the Palace of the Governors in 1698 for not properly turning over his office as Governor of New Mexico to his successor Don Pedro Rodriguez Cubero. He was eventually exonerated and honored in Spain for his previous exploits. In April of 1704, de Vargas died in Bernalillo, probably of dysentery. But his spirit lives on, and in June of 2007 a statue of him was dedicated in Cathedral Park.

Spanish settlements grew as people returned to their isolated farms and villages following the Pueblo Revolt. As families expanded through marriage and birth, the settlements gradually enlarged. From time to time new families joined on communal land grants and honored the village's founder by adapting his or her family name for their cluster of houses—the origin of many village names throughout the state. Farming was the main occupation, but adobe brick makers, weavers, tailors, carpenters and other artisans helped to make the city self-sufficient. Education suffered because farmers and craftspeople needed their children working alongside of them.

Other changes that took place after the Pueblo Revolt greatly affected life in New Mexico. Spanish slavery-like practices were abolished, and the Indian people were no longer persecuted for their religious activities. Unlike most other Native Americans, the Pueblo Indian people have been able to keep their languages, religions and customs alive on their ancestral homelands.

Santa Fe grew and prospered as a city. Under pressure from raids by nomadic tribes and bloody skirmishes with the neighboring Comanches, Apaches and Navajos, the Spanish settlement formed an alliance with the neighboring Pueblo Indians and maintained a successful religious and civil policy of peaceful coexistence. Although a few small skirmishes still took place, the Spanish and Pueblo populations became more cooperative with each other, working together to survive in a sometimes unforgiving landscape and against such common enemies as the Apaches and the Navajos. This cooperation was the origin of New Mexico's unique multicultural society.

The Mexican Republic (1821-1846)

Mexico won independence from Spain in 1821, and New Mexico became a province of the new republic. Santa Fe became the capital of the province of New Mexico. Many changes took place in the city during this time.

One of the most important was legalization of foreign trade, which led to the opening of the Santa Fe Trail. An American, William Becknell, was given permission to start a trade route from Missouri to Santa Fe. The trail wagons unloaded in front of the Palace of the Governors, carrying goods such as kilned brick, glass, textiles, whiskey, etc., things that Santa Feans were eager to acquire. American trappers and traders moved into the region. The Santa Fe Trail operated from 1821 to 1880, when the railroad came in and the trail was no longer needed.

The best-known Mexican governor during this occupation was Manuel Armijo, who served three separate terms (1827-29, 1837-44 and 1845-46). Known by the Mexicans as a firm administrator as well as charming, tough, and clever, Armijo was conversely known to Americans as a greedy and lustful tyrant and coward.

Mexicans created a more open society than the Spanish had. It was more democratic and had a unique spirit of independence. Women, especially, had much more independence. They had their own businesses and dealt cards in games of Monte. They could rent property, own livestock, keep their own wages and retain their maiden names. This was quite a startling difference from the status of American women of that time. One such woman was Gertrudes Barcelo, an aggressive, independent Mexican woman. Known as La Dona Tules, she ran a bar and gambling saloon on West Palace Avenue. Said to be the mistress of Governor Armijo, she was quite wealthy and was known to have given large sums of money to the church. She died in 1852 and is buried in the Basilica Cathedral of Saint Francis.

As time went on, the Mexican government began more and more to neglect New Mexico, an outpost far from Mexico City. Problems and violence arose as a result. Armijo was confirmed as governor again in 1838, but ordered to resign in 1844 because of cowardice during a confrontation against the newly independent Texans near the Arkansas River. He was restored as governor once again in 1845, shortly before the United States declared war on Mexico.

In August of 1846, General Stephen Watts Kearny, and his "Army of the West" marched closer to Santa Fe. Governor Armijo, after much consideration, left Santa Fe without defending it and marched his troops towards Mexico. In Mexico City he was tried for treason but acquitted. He did return to New Mexico and died there in 1853.

On August 18, 1846, Kearny led his 1500-man army into Santa Fe and raised the American flag over the Plaza. He was met with no opposition, only sullen faces and nervous anticipation from the mainly Mexican population. The new president of the United States, North Carolinian James K. Polk, believed that it was America's God-given right to own all the land to the Pacific Ocean. This doctrine was known as "Manifest Destiny."

As Walter Nugent states in his book *Habits of Empire*, ". . . Manifest Destiny had its belief as far back as the Puritan conviction that they, the Puritans, were "exceptional" people chosen by Providence—Nature's God—to occupy, settle and exploit the great expanses of North America." General Kearny's army was designated to carry out this expansion and extend United States influence towards California. It was this point of view, plus Mexico's unwillingness to accept Texas' independence and eventual annexation to the U.S. in 1845, that helped lead to the Mexican-American War. In 1848, Mexico signed the Treaty of Guadalupe Hidalgo, ceding New Mexico and California to the United States.

U.S. Territorial Period (1845-1912)

General Kearny immediately set out to establish authority in Santa Fe by selecting a site for a fort. He chose one close to the Plaza that commanded a view of the entire town, and here he built and named Fort Marcy for the Secretary of War, William L. Marcy. Eventually the earthwork fort fell into disrepair and literally disappeared. The United States maintained a garrison in Santa Fe until 1894.

The buildings that predominated at this time were the Palace of the Governors on the Plaza; the Exchange Hotel (now La Fonda Hotel) on San Francisco Street; the Paroquia where St. Francis Cathedral now stands; the Sena Hacienda on East Palace Avenue and "grand houses" on Grant Avenue and Griffin Street.

In 1851, Archbishop Jean B. Lamy arrived in Santa Fe. Eighteen years later, he began construction of the Saint Francis Cathedral. He was the model for the leading character in Willa Cather's 1927 fiction book, *Death Comes for the Archbishop*.

The Civil War briefly touched the area. For a few days in March 1862, the Confederate flag of General Henry Sibley flew over Santa Fe, until his forces were defeated by Union troops at the Battle of Glorieta Pass, often referred to as the "Gettysburg of the West." With the arrival of the telegraph in 1868 and the coming of the Atchison, Topeka and Santa Fe Railroad in 1880, Santa Fe and New Mexico underwent an economic revolution.

In 1909, it was decided that the Palace of the Governors was to be remodeled to become the History Museum of New Mexico. Jesse Nussbaum, an anthropologist, photographer, and eventually the first superintendent of Mesa Verde National Park, received the job of restoring the building. Using posts and *corbels* embedded in old walls as inspiration, he returned the building to its original Spanish-Pueblo look, calling it Pueblo Revival style. Today, when you think of a Santa Fe building, that style comes to mind.

Another architectural style part of Santa Fe today is Territorial style. This type of architecture began around 1850 when the Santa Fe Trail wagons were bringing in kilned brick from Missouri. It was cost prohibitive to bring in enough to build an entire house, so people with money bought a smaller number of bricks and bordered the roofs of their new homes with them, laying them out in a decorative style. They brought in milled lumber as well to build large Greek Revival windows and in some cases balconies. Today Pueblo Revival and Territorial styles dominate Santa Fe.

New Mexico was a United States territory from 1848 to 1912. What took us so long to become a state? Two main reasons come to mind. First, because we didn't have any gold or silver, we appeared quite worthless to those in Congress. Supposedly, Union General Sherman came to New Mexico after the Civil War and suggested it be sold back to Mexico for $500,000. Moreover, Congressional members were mainly of British ancestry, educated and Protestant. Their concept of New Mexico was as a wasteland with a population of Indians and Catholics. Finally, however, on January 6, 1912, New Mexico was named the 47th State.

Today New Mexico is the second largest producer of natural gas in the country; the state also produces oil and mines many minerals, including uranium. Hollywood has filmed a number of movies in New Mexico, including the Robert Redford classic *The Milagro Bean Field War, No Country for Old Men, Wild Hogs, The 3:10 to Yuma* and *Silverado*. In 2008, they started calling New Mexico "Tamalewood" because of over 100 movies filmed here in the past five years.

Santa Fe as a Creative Center

Native American Influences: From the makers of the early petroglyphs to the Pueblo pot makers, basket makers and weavers who felt the urge to adorn their wares, Native Americans have been at the forefront of creativity in New Mexico. Present day Pueblo folk artists work largely in pottery and art, exemplified by world famous Maria and Julian Martinez with their black-on-black pottery; painters Pop Chalee and Pablita Velarde, who painted Pueblo scenes from her childhood. She was sponsored by the WPA during the Depression and commissioned to paint murals for Bandelier National Monument.

In the 1960s, Native American contemporary painters such as R. C. Gorman, John Nieto, Lloyd Kiva New and T. C. Cannon came to the fore and helped make Santa Fe an important part of the international art market beginning in the 1970s.

Contemporary Native Americans such as Sherman Alexie, Leslie Marmon Silko and N. Scott Momaday are respected and well-read writers. Momaday won a Pulitzer Prize in 1969 for *House Made of Dawn.*

From the early days to the present, Native American craftspeople have been producing exquisite jewelry of silver, turquoise, coral, various other stones and a variety of materials including shells, feathers and beads. Under the *Portal* at the Palace of the Governors, you can find some of the finest examples and enjoy buying directly from the artists themselves. If you wish to see what is likely the most outstanding show of Native American art in the country, be sure to attend the annual SWAIA Indian Market held on the plaza every August.

Spanish Influences: New Mexico has also always had a strong Hispanic artistic tradition. *Santeros*, painters of *retablos*, weavers, furniture makers, potters, silversmiths and tinsmiths have all contributed their artistic skills. Rafael Aragon was an accomplished *santero* and painter. Silversmith Rodrigo Lorenzo lived in Santa Fe in 1639. Bernardino Sena, a blacksmith, came to Santa Fe in 1693, and he and his family operated a shop for well over 200 years. Nicolas Gabriel Ortega was born in Chimayó in 1729 and became the first of a long line of weavers in that family, and *santero* Jose Dolores Lopez carved but did not paint his *bultos*, a style still being done in Cordova, a town on the high road to Taos. Carlos Vierra, one of the first Hispanic artists to come here, painted the murals that are in St. Francis Auditorium of the New Mexico Museum of Art.

Present day Hispanic artists are still carrying on the creative tradition. Charlie Carrillo, Luis Tapia and Marie Romero Cash are all renowned woodcarvers, sometimes using contemporary themes. The late Eliseo and Paula Rodriguez revived the art of straw appliqué on wood, and Irvin Trujillo of Chimayó has brought back older weaving styles. The Spanish Market in July is an ideal venue to view and purchase examples of these arts.

Anglo Influences: Some Anglo writers and artists were living in Santa Fe prior to 1900. For example, General Lew Wallace, a territorial governor in 1878, was here when he completed the last part of his book *Ben Hur: A Tale of the Christ*, which became world famous and was turned into a movie with Charlton Heston in the 1950s. In the early 1900s, tuberculosis brought many creative people to Santa Fe. The city had two sanatoriums, one behind Cathedral Park and run by the Church and the Sunmount on Old Santa Fe Trail. One of these TB-afflicted artists, Sheldon Parsons, stayed on and became the first manager of the Museum of Fine Arts. Also settling here because of TB was Alice Corbin Henderson, a poet, along with her artist husband, William Penhallow Henderson. Their home became a gathering spot for artists and writers. Dorothy McGibbin, although not an artist, stayed in Santa Fe after being cured of the disease and eventually ran the Santa Fe office of the Manhattan Project (the top-secret project developing the Atomic Bomb) from 1943-1963.

Many well-known artists and writers lived in or spent time in Santa Fe, drawn by its natural beauty and cultural attributes. Among these were poet

Witter Bynner, writers D. H. Lawrence, Mary Austin and Pulitzer Prize winner Willa Cather. Other authors who spent time in Santa Fe included Pulitzer Prize winner Oliver LaFarge (*Laughing Boy*), Frank Waters (many books on Indians and early Spanish settlers) and Paul Horgan (writings about the Rio Grande and Archbishop Lamy).

Santa Fe has long been known as a leading American art colony. A leading influence in the formation of the early art scene was a group of five men referred to as Los Cinco Pintores, who captivated the locals in the 1920s. These were Fremont Ellis, Josef Bakos, Walter Mruk, Willard Nash and Will Shuster. Settling off Canyon Road on the Camino del Monte Sol, they built their own houses as best they could, considering their lack of carpentry skills. They were aptly nicknamed "the five nuts in five adobe huts" by the locals.

Artist Frank Applegate and writer Mary Austin started the Spanish Colonial Arts Society in 1925. Other artists who made the Santa Fe area home for some time include Georgia O'Keeffe, Robert Henri, John Sloan, Marsden Hartley and Randall Davey. Davey's home is now the Audubon Society on Upper Canyon Road. Today Santa Fe continues to be at the forefront of art. With over 250 galleries, it is considered the third leading art capital of the country after New York City and Los Angeles.

Right: The Portal of the Palace of the Governors.
An ideal place to buy authentic quality Indian jewelry and art.

THE DOWNTOWN WALKING TOUR OF OLD SANTA FE

Many old buildings in downtown Santa Fe have significant historical importance. In recognition of this, they are listed in the Historic Santa Fe Registry. While walking about town, you will see plaques on the outside walls of those designated as historic sites worthy of preservation. historicsantafe.com/Registry.html

BEGIN AT THE PLAZA

The Plaza: The Center of Social Life

The Plaza site was laid out by decree from King Philip II of Spain, a decree that applied to the construction of any town in the New World. King Philip II desired that all towns grow out symmetrically from a central gathering place.

Called La Plaza de Armas in the 17th century, the Plaza hosted military parades and religious festivals and eventually became the center of commerce and social life in Santa Fe. In the beginning, it was surrounded by a wall to keep enemies out, and at one time it housed a bullring. During the 19th Century a decorative gazebo featured band concerts. A new Victorian Style gazebo built with private funding several years ago now stands in the Plaza. Its roof is copper and you'll notice that the copper does not oxidize and turn green; instead it turns dark brown because of our low humidity. The new bandstand is the center of much activity during the summer, with concerts, dance events and local doings emanating from it. The trail route of the *Camino Real*, upon which wagons carried supplies from Mexico City (1598-1821), and the Santa Fe Trail (1821-1880) ended at the Plaza, where wares were unloaded and sold.

The obelisk in the center of the Plaza is a monument erected in 1868 to commemorate local soldiers, including the heroes of the Civil War from the battles of Valverde, Glorieta, Cañon de Apache, Pigeon's Ranch and Peralta. These 1862 battles were against the Confederate armies that briefly occupied Santa Fe and Albuquerque while on their way to attempt to reach the Colorado gold fields. The Confederates had hoped to use the gold to help subsidize their war effort and, possibly, to open a seaport in San Francisco. They never made it to their destination, and this was one important turning point of the war. The obelisk also honors men who died in campaigns against Indians.

Directly across from the Palace of the Governors sat a beautifully decorated adobe military chapel, La Castrense, once used by the soldiers but no longer there. The only remaining chapel artifact is a stone altar screen preserved at the Cristo Rey Church where Canyon Road meets Camino Cabra. Its centerpiece is *Santiago* or St. James, the patron saint of Spain.

In the 1600s most of the buildings surrounding the Plaza were military ones. During the 1800s shops began to appear. From 1860 to the late 1800s, young Jewish boys who had immigrated from Hamburg, Germany, opened retail businesses all around the Plaza. Most of these buildings featured Victorian architecture. Only one remains, the Catron Block on the corner of East Palace and Old Santa Fe Trail.

The Palace of the Governors:
The History Museum of New Mexico
palaceofthegovernors.org

The Palace of the Governors, most likely begun in 1609-10, is the oldest continuously occupied government building in the United States. Designed by the Spanish conquistadors under the direction of Governor Pedro de Peralta, it was one of several government buildings, or *casas reales*. It later became known as the Palace of the Governors.

The building was constructed with adobe bricks—compositions made of mud, sand, water, straw and sometimes dried manure. Adobe hardens to a very tough consistency and lasts a long time; some old adobe walls are still visible inside the building.

Adobe bricks originated in the Middle East. The use of adobe spread to Spain when the Moors occupied that country from 711 to 1491. In the early 8th century, Arabs had overrun northern Africa and converted the population to Islam, creating the people we know as the Moors, who went on to conquer Spain. They settled primarily in a part of the Iberian Peninsula they called Al Andalus. Today we call it Andalusia. While the rest of Europe was shrouded in the Dark Ages, the Moors were the cultured intellectuals of the time. They were the doctors, astronomers, architects, mathematicians (the creation of algebra is credited to them) and librarians. They taught the Spanish how to make archways and decorative tile. Words like alcohol, elixir, syrup, tac, zero, zenith, ginger, lilac, lemon, rhubarb and coffee are all derived from the Arabic language.

The Spanish conquistadors brought the adobe brick construction method to Santa Fe, where it was perfectly suited to the high-desert climate and the clay soils. The Pueblo Indians had been building their dwellings for many years with adobe, but not in brick form. Instead, they added successive layers of wet clay to the tops of walls, letting the clay dry, then adding more. This was known as puddle adobe. So the Spanish taught the Indians the adobe brick method and in return the Indians passed on their roof building method to the Spanish. This consisted of using *vigas* or tree trunks to hold up the roof and *latillas* or small twigs between the *vigas* to keep the roof itself (dirt) from falling into the rooms.

The Palace of the Governors has had many incarnations. Beginning as a fort, it was also a home to farmers, traders, missionaries and soldiers. The Supreme Court met in the Chapel; Territorial governors lived in the building prior to the adoption of statehood in 1912; and the Territorial Legislature met inside its walls.

At left, the Inn of the Anasazi done in Pueblo Revival Style and,
at right, The Burrito Company café done in Territorial Style.
These are the predominant architectural styles in Santa Fe.

At one time, part of the building was a post office and part of it was a prison. In fact, in 1807, Lt. Zebulon Pike (of Pike's Peak fame) was incarcerated there by the Spanish when New Mexico was still a Spanish territory.

The grounds housed much livestock, various stables, numerous gardens and a spring offering a natural water supply. It is thought that, early on, the grounds extended several blocks to the north.

In 1909, Jesse Nussbaum, a photographer and archaeologist, was given the huge undertaking of turning the Palace of the Governors into the New Mexico History Museum, which he completed by 1912. He is credited with restoring the Pueblo look to the Palace—what he called Pueblo Revival and we know today as "Santa Fe Style"—a look that became the predominant format for most local buildings.

EAST PALACE AVENUE & DOWNTOWN

The art gallery on the corner of East Palace and Washington Avenues was a gasoline station in the days-of-old (pre-1937) Route 66. Cars used the *portal* in front to pull in and "fill 'er up."

Trujillo Plaza
109 East Palace Avenue

This building and courtyard was the office of the Atomic Energy Commission from 1943 to 1963. Here scientists were processed for the highly secretive Manhattan Project during World War II. They were then transported to Los Alamos, where everyone had the same mailing address of P. O. Box 1663, Santa Fe, New Mexico. Children born in Los Alamos at that time—and there were 173 of them—have P. O. Box 1663, Sandoval County, N.M. on their birth certificates as their place of birth. In today's world this is a badge of some distinction.

When they arrived in Santa Fe, the scientists' wives were not enamored of the town, which in the early forties had almost no restaurants, close to nothing in the

The plaque marking the building where the scientists who worked on the atomic bomb got their papers before they went to Los Alamos.

The Shed Restaurant in Prince Plaza where Northern New Mexican food has been served since 1953.

way of shopping opportunities and only one movie theater, the Lensic. Little did they realize that Los Alamos had far fewer amenities!

Prince Plaza
113H East Palace Avenue

Originally, the small courtyard that now houses The Shed restaurant was the home, built in 1692, of a French Canadian trader, Antoine Roubidoux. In 1879, Bradford Prince, a Territorial Governor and Supreme Court Justice, moved in and lived there until 1919.

Sena Plaza
125 East Palace Avenue
visitsantafe.com/businesspage.cfm?businessid=1947
visitsantafe.com/businesspage.cfm?BusinessID=1281

This romantic hacienda and courtyard was once home to the Sena family of Santa Fe. The complex, over 200 years old now, was originally purchased by Juan Sena. He and his wife had 21 children, so clearly the hacienda began to grow. His son, José, eventually enlarged it to 33 rooms, including a second-story ballroom! When the Territorial Capitol burned down in 1892, the Legislature temporarily convened here.

Cathedral Park

Crossing over East Palace onto Cathedral Place, we pass some pillars and a gate that used to be the entry to the old St. Vincent Sanatorium, built in 1911 to care for victims of tuberculosis. The land around that entry is now called Cathedral Park.

At the eastern end of the Park is the Cuarto Centenario Monument, built in memory of the first Spanish colonists, friars and soldiers who came to the area in 1598. Erected in 2003, the monument depicts tools used at that time as well as the animals that were part of people's lives so long ago. It was sculpted by Donna Quastoff, who also created a statue a statue of Don Diego de Vargas, which was placed in the park and dedicated on June 3, 2007.

The Basilica Cathedral of St. Francis of Assisi
213 Cathedral Place
en.wikipedia.org/wiki/Cathedral_Basilica_of_Saint_Francis_of_Assisi
evanderputten.org/special/newmexico/sfcathedral.htm

Before the cathedral was built, four adobe churches stood in that same spot. The fourth was destroyed during the 1680 Pueblo Revolt and was replaced by La Parroquia (parish church), built between 1714 and 1717.

When Bishop Jean Baptiste Lamy, the first bishop of Santa Fe, arrived in 1851, he was shocked when he saw the fourth church. He felt that Santa Fe was the seat of the Archdiocese and, thus, Canon Law required that such a church be constructed of stone. The existing church was made of adobe and stucco in the Spanish Colonial style. He was determined to build a new and vibrant church in the French Romanesque style that he felt was closer to his idea of a proper Cathedral. Lamy and architects from his native France designed the cathedral; the cornerstone was laid in 1869 and the building completed in 1886. Note that the steeples normally seen on cathedrals aren't present: the archbishop ran out of funds.

The bishop brought over Italian stonecutters to quarry blocks of yellow

*Left: Cuarto Centenario Monument in Cathedral Park sculpted by
Donna Quastoff.
Right: A life-size statue (all 5'2" of him) of General deVargas in Cathedral Park.*

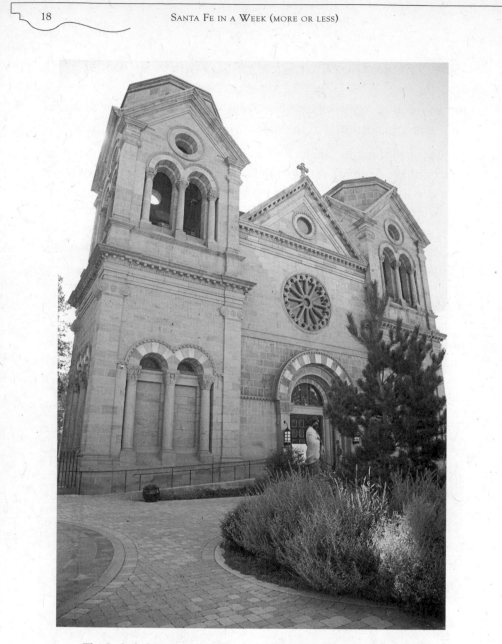

*The Cathedral Basilica of St. Francis of Assisi. Its cornerstone was laid in
1869 and the cathedral completed in 1886.*

limestone from a site miles from Santa Fe. That sleepy little town, now named
Lamy, is the main local Amtrak train stop.

    The cathedral was built around the old Parroquia, and after the walls were
up, the old church was demolished and the adobe blocks used as landfill in

front of the new church. However, the bishop did preserve a section of the old church that today houses La Conquistadora—also known *Nuestra Señora de la Paz* (Our Lady of Peace)— a small willow statue that is considered to be the oldest Madonna in the United States. Carved in the 1400s in Spain, she was brought to Mexico in 1625 and then transported to Santa Fe. She is also known as Our Lady of the Assumption and Our Lady of the Rosary.

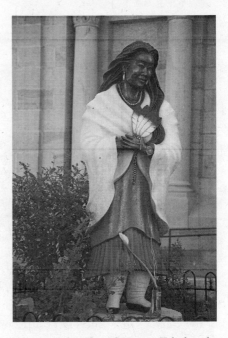

Statue of the Blessed Kateri Tekakwitha, the first Indian woman to be considered for sainthood.

In addition to the cathedral, Bishop Lamy built Santa Fe's first girls' school (run by the Sisters of Loretto) and the first boys' school, St. Michael's (which was originally on Old Santa Fe Trail) as well as 45 additional churches in New Mexico. Appointed an archbishop, Lamy has been immortalized in a book by Willa Cather, *Death Comes for the Archbishop*, published in 1927.

The cathedral was officially elevated to a basilica by Pope Benedict XVI on October 4, 2005.

La Fonda
100 East San Francisco Street
lafondasantafe.com

Directly across from the cathedral sits La Fonda, Santa Fe's oldest hotel. Its story parallels much of Santa Fe's history. It began in 1600 as a *fonda*, or inn, when Señor Alarid's family home was turned into a place for traders to stay. It then became the United States Hotel (1846-48), and afterwards, until 1919, the Exchange Hotel.

The present day La Fonda (The Inn) was built in 1924 on the site of the former hotel. Mary Jane Colter, an architect and decorator who devised El Tovar and the Phantom Ranch in the Grand Canyon, designed the interior, including the furniture and the lamps. The hotel was owned and operated by Fred Harvey,

La Fonda Hotel. Built in 1924 and originally run by Fred Harvey and his "Harvey Girls."

who was renowned throughout the West as a concessionaire and as the creator of the Harvey Girls concept of courteous, intelligent and impeccably neat waitresses.

Many famous people signed La Fonda's guest register, among them Colonel John Fremont, General and Mrs. Ulysses S. Grant and President and Mrs. Rutherford B. Hayes. More modern well-known guests included Lily Pons, Salvador Dali, Elliott Roosevelt and Lord and Lady Halifax.

In 1968, Sam Ballen bought the hotel and until his death in 2007 continued to upgrade and modernize it while preserving its traditional Southwestern look.

Water Street
sfaol.com/history/bishop.html

After you pass the cathedral, turn west onto Water Street and look behind you. You'll glimpse a portion of Archbishop Lamy's garden, a horticultural delight far more extensive in his day. The archbishop was an avid gardener and exchanged much gardening information with Flora Spiegelberg, wife of one of the German Jewish merchants in town. Because she spoke Latin, he asked her to teach catechism to his young Catholic parishioners, and she agreed to do so. Those interactions were but one fine example of people needing each other and working together in the frontier town of Santa Fe.

Water Street was so named because of the occasional overflow onto that street from the Santa Fe River. It is said that raw sewage sometimes ran down the street, then named the Rio Chiquito (1880s), and that this disastrous occurrence continued occasionally into the 1920s. It was hardly the charming place to walk that it is today.

We continue walking down Water Street, turning south onto Old Santa Fe Trail, the route taken into town by the wagon trains traveling from Missouri.

Loretto Chapel
207 Old Santa Fe Trail
orettochapel.com
hotelloretto.com

Our Lady of Light (Loretto) Chapel was built between 1873 and 1878 by the same Italian stonecutters who built St. Francis Cathedral. Modeled after the Sainte-Chapelle Church in Paris, it is a small, lovely chapel now privately owned and frequently used for weddings and concerts. The land next to it, currently occupied by the Inn at Loretto, was until 1968 home to the Loretto Academy for Girls. A statue of Our Lady of Lourdes stands atop the chapel.

The chapel gained fame for the spiral staircase built within and the mysterious, mystical story about the workman who constructed it. Originally, the chapel had no staircase to the choir loft. A staircase was needed, and the nuns made countless novenas to St. Joseph asking for his help. As the story goes, a carpenter arrived one day and agreed to assist. He fashioned an amazing circular

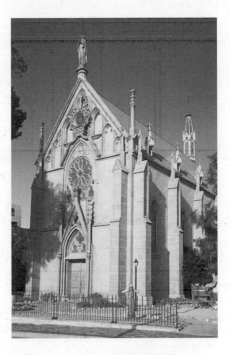

The famous Loretto Chapel, home of the "Miraculous Staircase"—with two 360-degree turns and thirty-three steps, it seems to float in the air.

staircase with two 360-degree turns and no center support, and then left without being paid. The nuns thought that the carpenter was in fact St. Joseph. Present-day historians attribute the work to Francois-Jean Rochas of Vif, Isere, France, but the legend of St. Joseph still captures the imagination. The mystery of the staircase has been the subject of television programs, including *Unsolved Mysteries*, and *The Staircase*, a dramatic television presentation on the subject.

Walking along the Old Santa Fe Trail (1821-1880) we pass the Inn at Loretto, built in 1975 in the Pueblo style. Look down at the Santa Fe River while crossing West Alameda Street. It's a dry river most of the year, except during spring runoff.

OLD EAST DE VARGAS STREET AREA

Barrio de Analco

East De Vargas Street marks the beginning of the Barrio de Analco, or "district on the other side of the river." Next to the Plaza, this is the oldest settlement of European origin. It was actually constructed by Tlaxcalan Indians brought

The San Miguel Mission 1610 was both a mission and a fort.

from Mexico as servants by the Spanish and the Franciscan Missionaries.

San Miguel Mission
401 Old Santa Fe Trail

The San Miguel Mission, built around 1610, was perhaps the first church in the United States, thus it is also known as the "Oldest Church." During the Pueblo Revolt of 1680 (the only successful revolt of its kind in the United States), the Indians burned the roof of the church.

After the Spanish regained control of Santa Fe in 1693, they set about restoring the mission, work that was completed around 1710. This time it became a fortress, with new outer walls, and added battlements to the roof. No further battles oc-curred, and by the 1800s the church had again been altered to include a triple-tiered tower. It was changed one more time, in 1870, to its current square tower configuration.

In 1798, an altar screen was added to include the impressive gilded statue of St. Michael, the patron saint of the Franciscan brothers. It was brought from Mexico in 1709 and was carried around New Mexico to help raise money for the rebuilding of the church.

evanderputten.org/special/newmexico/sanmiguel.htm

Oldest House in Santa Fe
215 East De Vargas Street
tedmontgomery.com/santafe/#top

Based on Adolph Bandelier's study that the foundation of this house dates back to a pueblo (circa 1250 CE), and the *vigas* reveal their age as coming from the 1740 to 1767 timeframe, this would support the house's claim to being the oldest house in town. Some believe this is actually the oldest standing house in the U.S.A. Whether or not this is true, it certainly is one of the oldest. The interior is a stunning example of Spanish colonial times, with its remaining dirt floor, corner fireplace, and traditional *viga* and *latilla* ceiling.

The Oldest House, *certainly one of the oldest houses in Santa Fe.*

Santa Fe Playhouse
142 East De Vargas Street
santafeplayhouse.org

This unique theater was incorporated in 1922 by well-known writer Mary Austin. In 1962, it moved into its present home, an adobe building with a late-1800s life as a livery stable followed by tenure as a blacksmith shop.

The Roque Tudesqui House
129-135 East De Vargas Street
historicsantafe.com/pop-tudesqui.html

The west section of this house was sold to Italian-born Roque Tudesqui, a Santa Fe Trail trader, sometime before 1841. The Territorial style house has three-foot-thick adobe walls and an outrageously beautiful 80-year-old wisteria vine.

The Gregorio Crespin House
132 East De Vargas Street
legis.state.nm.us/lcs

This homestead, built between 1720 and 1747, was part of the property owned by Gregorio Crespin and then sold to Bartolome Marquez for 50 pesos. The original land grant was given by General Vargas to Juan de Leon Brito, a Mexican Tlaxcalan Indian who, from 1692 to 1693, helped the Spanish reclaim Santa Fe from the Pueblo Indians.

At the end of the Barrio de Analco, you can catch a glimpse of the state Capitol building (built 1964-65). It is called the "Roundhouse," as it resembles an Indian *kiva* in its round shape. From the air, the New Mexican sun symbol adopted from the Zia Pueblo is visible.

BACK TOWARDS THE PLAZA

Turn right and walk down an alleyway toward the Santa Fe River. There is a walking path that parallels the river and East Alameda Street. Walk along this path, past the state Supreme Court until you come to Don Gaspar Avenue. Turn right on Don Gaspar and head back towards the Plaza. Formerly owned by Don Gaspar Ortiz y Alarid, this area was once an open field. Sr. Ortiz y Alarid lived in the northwest corner building at Don Gaspar and Water Street.

The Hotel St. Francis
210 Don Gaspar Avenue (and Water Street)
hotelstfrancis.com

Originally the site of the Palace Hotel (built in the 1880s), the building burned completely to the ground in 1922. In 1924, it was rebuilt and reopened as the De Vargas Hotel, a first-class hotel with a spacious lobby, a wonderful dining room and a bar. In the late 1920s, when Water Street was part of Route 66, the hotel was a favorite stopping-off

The Hotel St. Francis. The old DeVargas Hotel trans-formed into the elegant Hotel St. Francis.

place. Time took its toll, however, and the hotel was eventually sold in the 1980s and restored to its former Victorian glory, opening as the Hotel St. Francis. The St. Francis patio is a perfectly delightful spot for breakfast, lunch and dinner.

San Francisco Street
sfaol.com/history/street.html
byways.org/explore/byways/2065
lensic.com

One of the city's oldest streets, San Francisco Street was the final destination at the end of the *Camino Real* (the King's Road) for covered wagons completing their 1,600-mile-journey from Mexico City.

From the time the Spanish founded Santa Fe all goods came from Mexico City via the *Camino Real*. It was a long, hard and dangerous journey that ended as the wagons came up San Francisco Street and unloaded on the Plaza. Historian Mark Simmons pointed out the hazards in an article in *The Santa Fe New Mexican*:

The most dangerous stretch of the long *Camino Real* could be found in southern New Mexico. There it passed through the heart of Apacheria, as the homeland of the Apaches was called. Wagon trains expected to suffer casualties. In the Mesilla Valley one caravan, after an attack, buried its dead at trailside. The next batch of travelers, noting the cluster of new marked graves, referred to the site as El Jardin de Las Cruces (the Garden of the Crosses). Today's city of Las Cruces in its name continues to bear witness to that long-ago tragedy.

Further west on this street is the Lensic Theatre, built in 1930 as a legitimate theater and movie house. Rita Hayworth, Roy Rogers and Judy Garland all performed onstage at the Lensic. It was beautifully restored in 2001 and is now a prized venue for stage and dance venues, movies and lectures.

Burro Alley

An historic 17th-century street adjacent to the Lensic is Burro Alley, the area once used to hitch burros needed for bringing wood down from the mountains. It is now a pedestrian walkway. A mural depicting the burros was done in the 1940s by Howard Kretz Coluzzi.

Burros carried wood down from the Sangre de Cristo Mountains for hundred of years.

Felipe B. Delgado House
124 West Palace Avenue
historicsantafe.com/popdelgado.html

Continuing east on West Palace Avenue you will come to the Felipe B. Delgado House. Señor Delgado was a wealthy merchant in the wagon-train shipping business. After initially using this site as land to stable his mules, Delgado built his house here in 1890. Modified in the early 20th century, it remains an excellent

Burro Alley with the Burro Alley Café serving food alfresco.

example of local adobe construction, and it is authentically Territorial in style. It was used as a private residence until it was sold in 1970. It is currently occupied by a local bank.

New Mexico Museum of Art
107 West Palace Avenue

Diagonally across from the Delgado House stands the New Mexico Museum of Art, one of many superb museums in town. The Museum houses a collection of more than 20,000 works of art, including paintings, photography, sculpture and works on paper relating primarily to the American Southwest.

New Mexico Museum of Art displays works of Santa Fe and Taos masters, as well as contemporary exhibits.

The architecture firm of Rapp and Rapp constructed this building in Spanish Pueblo Revival style. Completed in 1917, it also houses the St. Francis Auditorium, designed to look like a pueblo church interior. The wall mural panels were done by Carlos Vierra (1876-1937), the first artist of any note to move here permanently (1904). Included in the Museum's permanent collection are works by such artists as Georgia O'Keeffe, Ernest Blumenschein and John Sloan.

Continuing to walk east on West Palace Avenue, you return to your starting point at the Palace of the Governors. Make sure you look at the window on the corner of Lincoln and Palace Avenues. The bars on these windows are made of gun barrels!

TOURS, TOURS, TOURS

As a museum guide for the Palace of the Governors and professional tour guide, I know the value of accurate, shared information, and I really recommend that you take at least one guided tour while you're here. The tour could focus on any number of personal interest areas such as history, art, architecture, Indian art and culture or ghosts. Plan on spending an hour or two with your guide.

WALKING AND CUSTOM TOURS

Historic Walks of Santa Fe
(505) 986-8388
historicwalksofsantafe.com

Historic Walks of Santa Fe offers a variety of types of tours. Some are given all year round, but some only May through October. Call for information. Some require reservations. This company was featured on "Good Morning America" and is the company for which I give tours.

Above: The author "lecturing" during a tour for Historic Walks of Santa Fe.

La Fonda Tours

- Daily from La Fonda (on Plaza) at 9:45 a.m. and 1:15 p.m.
- Daily from Plaza Galleria (on Plaza) at 10 a.m. and 1:30 p.m.
- Daily from the Hilton of Santa Fe at 10:15 a.m. and 1:45 p.m.
- $14 per person, children under 12 accompanied by adult are free, senior discount.

Eldorado Tours

- Daily from the Eldorado Hotel at 9:30 a.m. and 1:30 p.m.
- Daily from the St. Francis Hotel at 9:45 a.m. and 1:45 p.m.

Ghostwalker

The stories and legends of the ghosts of Santa Fe.
- Starts Friday from the Hilton at 5:30 p.m. and from La Fonda lobby at 6 p.m.
- $14 per person, reservations required.

"Signature" Spirit Walk

A more in-depth Ghostwalker tour where "spirits come alive."
- Starts Friday from La Fonda lobby at 6 p.m.
- Call for group rates, 8-10 minimum, reservations required.

Santa Fe Art Gallery Tours

Tour of galleries, New Mexico Museum of Art and the Georgia O'Keeffe Museum with an expert.

- Starts Friday from La Fonda lobby at 2 p.m.
- $30 per person (museum admission fees included).

Custom Canyon Road Art Walk

Tour of Canyon Road historic buildings and important galleries.
- Leaves from La Fonda lobby at 2 p.m.
- Call for details and pricing, reservations required.

Santa Fe Artists at Home

Special group tours to meet the artists of Santa Fe in their homes.
- Includes transportation, reservations required.
- Call for details and pricing.

Prestige Shopping Tour with Lunch

Half-day tour of some of Santa Fe's finest shops.
- Price includes lunch at one of downtown's outstanding restaurants.
- Reservations required, minimum of 4 people.
- $50 per person, includes lunch. $25 per person, without lunch.

Georgia O'Keeffe Museum Tour

Led by a professional guide and docent from the Georgia O'Keeffe Museum, including luncheon at the O'Keeffe Café.

- Call for pricing and advance reservations.

Out-of-Town and Special Events

Call about Bandelier, Taos, Chimayó, Abiquiú (O'Keeffe Country Tours and Santa Fe School of Cooking/Historical Tour)

- Destination planning for weddings, reunions and private groups.

For Children: Camp Santa Fe

Visit historicwalksofsantafe.com for details.

History Talks, Palace Walks
(Sponsored by the New Mexico History Museum)
(505) 476-5109

Walking tour of Downtown Santa Fe.

- Leaves from the blue gate of the Palace of the Governors on Lincoln Avenue.
- 10:15 a.m. to noon, Monday-Saturday, April-October.
- $10, children under 16 accompanied by adult, free.
- Fees donated to the Palace of the Governors.

New Mexico Museum of Art Walking Tour
107 West Palace Avenue
(505) 476-5072

Leaves from the museum steps at 107 West Palace Avenue every Monday at 10 a.m., May through August.

- This tour shows the art and architecture of the city.
- $10 per person, children under 16 accompanied by adult, free.

Santa Fe Detours
(800) detours or (505) 983-6565
sfdetours.com/tours.html

The Walking Tour of Santa Fe

Walking tour of historical downtown and the state capitol complex.
- Starts daily from the T-shirt tree at 107 Washington Avenue on the northeast corner of the Plaza at 9:30 a.m. and 1:30 p.m., 2-1/2-hour tour.
- $10 per person, $5 for children 12 and under.

Stefanie Beninato
A Well-Born Guide—Have Ph.D., Will Travel
(505) 988-8022
http://www.zianet.com/stebeni/santafetours2.htm

Women in NM History

A different downtown tour. Learn about the prominent and notorious women who lived in Santa Fe.
- Thursday at 1:30 p.m., or by appointment.
- $22 per person, minimum $56. Call for reservations.

Artists and Acequias: A Cultural and Artistic Tour of Canyon Road and the Eastside

Have you already seen the downtown but would like to find your way in one of the older and more scenic neighborhoods? Learn about the artists and writers who made Santa Fe one of the largest art markets in the U.S. See the mother ditch and find out about unique community events.

- $22 per person, minimum $56. Group rates available.
- Mondays at 10 a.m. or by appointment. Call for reservations.

Bars and Brothels of Santa Fe: A Red Light Tour

Check out the famous watering holes in town, both past and present.
- $22 per person, minimum $56.

- Wednesdays and Saturdays, 7:30-9 p.m. winter; 8:30-10 p.m. summer.
- Group rates available.

A Spirits Different Combo Tour

Does listening to ghost stories work up a thirst? Then come on this tour that combines visits to bars, brothels, haunted places, and sometimes all three in the same place! Stop at one of these spirited watering holes for a sip of spirits while on the tour.

- $30 per person, minimum $75. By appointment only.
- Group rates available. Call for reservations.

The Dark Side of Santa Fe: Ghosts, Mysteries & Legends

Learn about the ghosts in public or private buildings in this 400-year-old city.

- $16 per person, $10 children, minimum $40.
- Sunday, Thursday at 5:30 and 7:30 p.m., or by appointment.

A History Different: A Look at the Jewish Legacy in New Mexico

An overview tour of the Jewish whereabouts in the 19th century, the hidden or Crypto-Jews and the present-day Jewish community.

- $22 per person, minimum $56. Group rates available.
- Thursday at 10 a.m., or by appointment.

Garden Tours: Past & Present

Tour Santa Fe gardens in public buildings, galleries and private places with a local gardener and historian.

- $26 per person, minimum $65. Group rates available.
- Tuesday at 10 a.m., or by appointment.

Bread and Chocolate: An Artisanal Epicurean Delight!

Come on a unique tasting experience where you will enjoy sampling fresh breads and crêpes, as well as traditionally made cacao drinks and sumptuous chocolates from the kitchens of their creators. Get acquainted with the recently opened Railyard and glimpse the architectural diversity of the Don Gaspar Historic Neighborhood.

- $65 per person, minimum $140. Call for reservations.
- Fridays 10 a.m., or by appointment.

TOURS ON WHEELS

Custom Tours by Clarice
(505) 438-7116
santafecustomtours.com

- Daily at 10 a.m., 12 Noon, 2 p.m., 4 p.m.
- Reservations recommended
- $15 per person

The Loretto Line
(505) 983-3701
visitsantafe.com/businesspage.cfm?businessid=2308

- $15 per person, $6 per adult under 12 accompanied by adult

Santa Fe Detours City Tours
(800) DETOURS or (505) 983-6565
sfdetours.com/tours.html

- $10 per person for 1¼ hours
- $30 per person for three hours (includes admissions)

OUT OF TOWN TOURS

Great Southwest Adventures
(505) 455-2700
swadventures.com

Half-day or full-day tours led by guides who are experienced in the natural history, culture and ecology of the area. See website for details about each tour.

Bandelier National Monument

- Summer: $90, 5 hours.

Abiquiú and Georgia O'Keeffe Country

- Summer: $90, 5 hours.

Taos (includes Taos Pueblo and Rio Grand Gorge)

- Summer: $115, 8 hours.

New Mexico Sampler

- Tour Spanish and Pueblo cultures of New Mexico.
- $80, 4 hours.

Kasha-Katuwe Tent Rocks National Monument

- $85, 4 hours.

Chaco Canyon National Historic Park

- Minimum 4 guests at $150 each, all day (including lunch).
- Great Southwest Adventures also offers charter and group tours.

Santa Fe Detours Out-of-Town Tours
(800) detours or (505) 983-6565
sfdetours.com/tours.html

Half or full day tours, daily except Sunday.
- Reservations required, pickup available.

Taos

- $80 per person, children under 12 half price, all day.

Bandelier National Monument

- $70 per person, children under 12 half price, half day.

Puye Cliff Dwellings (includes Santa Clara Pueblo)

- $70 per person, children under 12 half price, half day.

Custom Tours

Hiking, biking, llama treks or private guides.
- Call to make arrangements.

Santa Fe Mountain Adventures
(505) 988-4000 or (800) 965-4010
santafemountainadventures.com

Out of doors adventure journeys for groups and families, including hiking, geocaching, rafting, horseback riding, mountain biking, fly fishing and snowshoeing. Explore the creative, cultural world as well, including cooking classes, pottery and historic tours. Call for more information and pricing.

Santa Fe Garden Club Home & Garden Tours
Behind Adobe Walls ®
(505) 984-0022, Westwind Travel.

- Summer bus tour of Santa Fe homes and gardens.
- The last Tuesday in July and the first Tuesday in August.
- $60 per person, reservations required.

Pequeño Tours
(505) 823-9030

Santa Fe home and garden tour.
- April through October.
- $45 per person, minimum of 10 people, reservations required.

Santa Fe Tours
(888) 839-3823
santafetours.net

Active tours of the Santa Fe area via helicopter, hot air balloon, horseback, rafting, sketchbook and train, including a special summertime train ride and barbecue. See website or call for information and reservations.

MUSEUM TOURS

Museum of New Mexico
(505) 827-6463
museumofnewmexico.org

Please see the chapter on museums for complete information regarding museum descriptions, hours of operation, museum entry fees, etc. The information given here relates strictly to the guided tours of each site. For updated information on the Museum of New Mexico, call their 24-hour information line or go to the main website for the Museum system.

New Mexico Museum of Art

107 West Palace Avenue
(505) 476-5072

nmartmuseum.org
- Docent tours: Tuesday-Sunday at 10:30 a.m. and 1:30 p.m.
- Tour fee is included with $9 museum admission

New Mexico History Museum and Palace of the Governors

105 West Palace Avenue
(505) 476-5100

palaceofthegovernors.org
- Docent tours: Tuesday-Sunday at 10:30 a.m., noon, 1:30 p.m., and 3 p.m.
- Tour fee is included with $9 museum admission

Museum of Indian Arts & Culture

710 Camino Lejo
(505) 476-1250

miaclab.org
- Docent tour: First Saturday of the month at 2 p.m.
- Tour fee is included with $9 museum admission

Museum of International Folk Art

706 Camino Lejo
(505) 476-1200

moifa.org
- Docent tour: Tuesdays and Wednesdays at 10:15 a.m. and 2 p.m.
- Thursdays through Sundays at 10:15 a.m., 1 p.m. and 3 p.m.
- Tour fee is included with $9 museum admission

DIVAS AND DIVERSIONS

Richard Bradford (1933-2002), author of *Red Sky at Morning*, once said of Santa Fe: "At age 12, within 15 minutes of coming here, I realized that I'd been making a terrible mistake living in large urban centers. This was the place for me. I felt immediately at home; I have never felt so quickly, so comfortably, so deeply attracted." (From *Turn Left at the Sleeping Dog*, by John Pen la Farge.)

Santa Fe is a town of incredible cultural diversity. We are thrilled to share world-class offerings in all kinds of music, including classical (opera, chamber music, orchestra and choral music), jazz, flamenco, country, bluegrass and world beat, as well as popular artists who come to entertain under the stars at our local outdoor venues in the summer. Santa Fe has its own stage shows and plays host to traveling theater groups as well as ballet, international and modern dance groups that come to town.

Above: The Emerson String Quartet with Emanuel Ax on piano, 2008. (Photo courtesy of the Santa Fe Chamber Music Festival.)

The John Crosby Theater at the Santa Fe Opera.
(Photo by Robert Reck/the Santa Fe Opera)

In addition to all our outstanding restaurants, we have a variety of other attractions, including a farmer's market that ranks with the best in the country, and a flea market where a myriad of items are sold at bargain prices.

- santafeartsandculture.org
- nmoca.org
- nmculture.org

SOME OF THE FINEST CLASSICAL MUSIC

Santa Fe Opera
Approximately 9 miles north of Santa Fe on U.S. 84/285.
(800) 280-4654 or (505) 986-5900
santafeopera.org

In 1980, my wife, Mary, and I came to Santa Fe for the first time. Although we were not opera fans, we had heard so much about the Santa Fe Opera that we got tickets for Mozart's *The Magic Flute*. I must say that being in the opera house, viewing the sunset over Los Alamos and watching the stars appear as the desert breeze wafted in while we listened to the overture was a truly delightful, multi-sensory experience. We became opera lovers that night.

Santa Feans have been treated to the opera since John Crosby inaugurated it in 1957. Mr. Crosby served as the company's general director from its founding in 1957 until 2000 when he retired. He passed on in 2002, at the age of 76. Famed soprano Leontyne Price said of the opera: "Once I discovered the Santa Fe Opera, I stopped going to Salzburg and Glyndebourne."

Situated on a former guest ranch nine miles north of Santa Fe, the opera house is acoustically perfect. Originally, there were 480 seats under the stars. 1998 saw the construction of a new 2,128-seat theater partially covered by a roof. Call for a schedule and tickets before you arrive in town, as most nights are sellouts. You can also order tickets from the opera website.

Although the season runs from late June to late August, some nights are cool and some seats are not fully covered. It is always wise to bring rain gear.

- Season: late June to late August.

Santa Fe Chamber Music Festival
208 Griffin Street, office
(505) 983-2075
For tickets only, in summer: (505) 982-1890
santafechambermusic.org
lensic.com

ticketssantafe.org

Since 1972 the Chamber Music Festival has been a mainstay of the classical music scene in Santa Fe. From mid-July to the end of August, the festival presents over forty concerts at St. Francis Auditorium and at the newly renovated Lensic Performing Arts Center, featuring world-class musicians such as Pinchas Zuckerman, Cho-Liang Lin and the Orion String Quartet.

Supplementing the evening concerts, one-hour noon concerts are presented at the St. Francis Auditorium for a cost of $15, students $5. These noon concerts are among the most popular recitals in Santa Fe.

In addition to traditional classical music, new "cutting edge" classical music is performed in the very contemporary SITE Santa Fe venue. Jazz and world music are also part of the programming of the festival.

- Performances at various venues.
- Season: mid-July to end of August.

Santa Fe Desert Chorale
(505) 988-2282 or (800) 244-4011
desertchorale.org

If you enjoy chorale music, you will love the Desert Chorale. Initiated in 1983, it represents the finest in chamber chorus singing. One evening, at the acoustically perfect Loretto Chapel, we listened to a mesmerizing blend of ancient Hebrew psalms and Gregorian chants that came off beautifully. The Chorale performs not only at the Loretto Chapel, but also at the Lensic Performing Arts Center, Santa María de la Paz Catholic Community and the St. Francis Cathedral.

- Performances at various venues
- Season: end of June to mid-August, then during Christmas season.

Santa Fe Pro Musica
211 West San Francisco Street
(800) 960-6680 or (505) 988-4640
santafepromusica.com

Santa Fe Pro Musica was established in 1994 to present classical concerts of the highest quality consistent with international standards of excellence. Locally based, Santa Fe Pro Musica provides both orchestral and chamber music offerings, specializing in music from the 19th century and before. Using its unique affiliation with the Smithsonian Institution, Santa Fe Pro Musica uses period instruments whenever possible. A complete schedule is available at its website.

- Performances at various venues
- Season: year round

Santa Fe Symphony and Chorus
551 West Cordova Road, Suite D, office
(800) 480-1319 or (505) 983-1414
sf-symphony.org

Santa Fe has its own symphony orchestra performing a variety of classical traditions from Handel and Beethoven to Dvorak and Copeland.

Some performances also showcase classical Spanish and jazz crossover styles. Call for schedule.

- Performances at the Lensic Performing Arts Center, 211 West San Francisco Street
- Season: year round

MUSICAL AND THEATRICAL OFFERINGS FOR EVERY TASTE

For more ideas, see the calendar of events.

Juan Siddi Flamenco Theatre Company

(888) 4-flamenco or (505) 955-8562

juansiddiflamenco.com

This company of professional dancers and musicians presents diverse and demanding performances of music and dance showcasing the rhythms of flamenco. Flamenco performers come from throughout the United States and Spain. It is recognized as one of the nation's leading performing arts groups,. Flamenco aims to preserve, strengthen and disseminate the rich and diverse artistic heritage of Spain, enriching the lives not only of people of Spanish ancestry, but of all Americans.

- Performances at the Lodge at Santa Fe, 750 North St. Francis Drive
- Season: late June to mid August

Santa Fe Playhouse

142 East De Vargas Street

(505) 983-4262

santafeplayhouse.org

Founded in 1922, the Santa Fe Playhouse is the oldest continuously running theater company west of the Mississippi. It is distinguished by being housed in an historic adobe building in the Barrio de Analco and is noted for the annual Fiesta Melodrama, a spoof and satire on the City Different. As was intended by founder Mary Austin, the Playhouse is dedicated to presenting works that give voice to Santa Fe's many cultures and communities. The Playhouse offers a variety of theater year round with musicals, comedies, dramas, murder-mysteries and classics.

Lensic Performing Arts Center
211 West San Francisco Street
Box office: (505) 988-1234
lensic.com

Originally opened in 1930 as a film and vaudeville palace, the Lensic Theatre was remodeled in 2000 and reopened as a world-class, state-of-the-art, 821-seat venue—an ideal space for chamber music, theater, modern dance, flamenco, ballet, jazz, operetta, film and poetry. Beautifully restored, the Lensic Performing Arts Center boasts perfect acoustics and "not a bad seat in the house." It is now the venue of choice for many local and national productions. You can check the Lensic website to find out what is happening during the week you plan to be in town. You cannot

The Lensic Center for the Performing Arts was remodeled in 2000 and gave Santa Fe the "stage" for the performing arts that was so needed.

purchase tickets from this site, but you can look at a seating chart and use one of the links provided to purchase tickets directly from the organization holding the performance. Or, of course, you can call the box office and purchase tickets there.

Piano Bar at Vanessie Restaurant
434 West San Francisco Street
(505) 982-9966
vanessiesantafe.com/pianobar.htm

Enjoy dinner or just stop by for dessert or a drink and enjoy live music from Santa Fe's only piano bar. Some of the patrons even get up to sing and dance!

OTHER VENUES FOR NATIONAL ACTS

Several other venues draw national music acts from rock to jazz to country. Check these Web sites to see who may be playing when you come to town. Also, check the newspapers and fliers about town for other venues as well as the club scene.

Journal Pavilion
Off I-25 south of Albuquerque
(505) 246-8742
journalpavilion.com

The large rock acts play here. It is easy to get to, just south of Albuquerque and about an hour from Santa Fe. The easiest way to go is to follow the directions on the Pavilion website. You will also find a schedule, and you can purchase tickets there as well.

Casinos

Many of the Indian casinos bring in name acts, Las Vegas style. They usually feature classic rock, country, comedy and nightclub acts. They advertise on their billboards, on TV and in the paper. You can also check the websites of the individual casinos offering events.

LET'S GO TO THE MOVIES

If you're a movie buff, you might want to take in a flick after dinner. Santa Fe is a movie town. It holds its own film festival every fall and many movies have been filmed in New Mexico (e.g., *The Milagro Bean Field War*, *Rent*, *Little Miss Sunshine*, *The Longest Yard*, *3:10 to Yuma*, *Wild Hogs*, *Due Date*, *True Grit* and *Thor*, just to mention several).

- For a long compilation of movies filmed in New Mexico, visit nmusa.com/nmfilms.

Theatres showing major releases from large studios and major independents

Regal Santa Fe Stadium 14
San Isidro Plaza
3474 Zafarano at Cerrillos
(505) 424-6296
regmovies.com (enter zip code 87505)

Fourteen-screen complex with stadium seating. Offers first-run features.

Regal Cinema North
North side of Santa Fe Place
(corner of Rodeo and Cerrillos Roads)
(505) 471-3377
regmovies.com (enter zip code 87505)

Offers first-run features on six screens.

Regal DeVargas 6
DeVargas Center, 562 North Guadalupe Street
(505) 988-2775
regmovies.com (enter zip code 87501)

Offers first-run American and foreign films from major and independent studios.

Theaters showing films from major, independent and foreign studios

CCA Cinematheque
Center for Contemporary Arts
1050 Old Pecos Trail
(505) 982-1338
ccasantafe.org/cinematheque.htm

Offers carefully-selected foreign and American films, including recent movies and revivals not found elsewhere.

Lensic Performing Arts Center
225 West San Francisco Street
(505) 988-1234
lensic.org

This spectacularly restored 1930 movie palace offers big screen classics from time to time.

The Screen
1600 St. Michael's Drive
(505) 473-6494
thescreen.csf.edu

The theatre at the Santa Fe University of Art and Design's Greer Garson Communication Center. Shows foreign, independent and restored films.

OTHER UNIQUE DIVERSIONS

Santa Fe Farmers' Market
430 West Manhattan Street, in the Railyard Park
(near train depot off Guadalupe Street)
Call for market days. (505) 983-4098
santafefarmersmarket.com

*The Farmers' Market at the Railyard. The flavor and
warmth of Santa Fe can be found while shopping this
wonderful locally grown food market.*

This unique year-round farmers' market now in its new building had
its beginnings in 1976. *Sunset Magazine* named it one of the best in the
Southwest. Hispanic growers, whose land has been in their families for
centuries, bring apples, chiles, vegetables, salsa and jams to the market.
They stand alongside young Anglo farmers who love the land as well and
harvest their bounty for all of us. Most of the market sellers are certified
organic growers. During harvest time, the market is buzzing at 7 a.m. with
coffee and pastry vendors at the ready to satisfy early shoppers. Bands, guitar players and country violins appear on a catch-as-catch-can basis. Here
at the market you meet the residents of Santa Fe, so don't be surprised if
you're invited to someone's home for drinks that night.

Tesuque Pueblo Flea Market
About 9 miles north of Santa Fe on
U.S. 84/285 near the Opera
(505) 995-8626
tesuquepuebloffleamarket.com

Called Trader Jack's when it first opened in the 1980s, the flea market has grown each year. Now run by the Tesuque Pueblo on its land, it offers a fascinating mix of merchandise sold by equally fascinating individuals. In the stalls of the 200 permanent vendors, you'll find both Native

The start of Canyon Road. Walk, don't drive this "art" street that was originally an Indian foot path. At the top, pick a restaurant for a drink or lunch.

American and contemporary jewelry, clothing, oriental rugs, antiques, woodwork, furniture, local food, jams, salsa, art, photography and more. Wear sunglasses, a hat and some comfortable, closed walking shoes.

• Open every Friday, Saturday and Sunday.

Canyon Road Walk
canyonroadarts.com

All the guidebooks and travel agents tell you to make sure you walk Canyon Road to see the art galleries. Thankfully, Canyon Road has survived its onslaught of tourists and has not become a "theme" street devoid of sensibility.

Canyon Road has gone through its own realities, first as a Pueblo Indian footpath, then as a road the Spanish called *El Camino de Cañon* (Canyon Road). Spaniards built modest homes here early in the 20th century, and artists migrated to the road because of its low rent and pleasant vistas.

Interspersed among private adobe residences, art galleries and shops, occasional restaurants or coffee shops in several historic houses provide lunches and fine dining.

Every Friday evening many of the galleries on Canyon Road hold show openings. This Friday night walk is an enjoyable way to see the art, meet the artists, and enjoy refreshments in the cool Santa Fe evening.

Another special Canyon Road walk is held every year on Christmas Eve. Brightly burning *farolitos* line Canyon Road and several side streets, as thousands of Santa Feans walk and mingle about, enjoying the holiday decorations, greeting friends and singing carols. Bonfires and hot apple cider warm bodies and souls. The smell of the burning piñon logs will forever linger in your memory. Be sure to dress warmly.

First Ward School
400 Canyon Road

Once in a while you come across a Santa Fe building that is neither Pueblo Revival nor Territorial style, and you may ask "What style is it?" The First Ward School is constructed of kilned brick rather than adobe and is of the Neoclassical style. It was built as a public school house in

First Ward School on Canyon Road. Originally built as a schoolhouse, it sports a "witch's hat" as part of the roof.

1906 to someday replace the Loretto and St. Michael schools built by Archbishop Lamy, but in fact it never did. Twenty-two years after the school's completion, the city sold it. It has undergone several incarnations and is now one of the many art galleries on Canyon Road.

El Zaguan
545 Canyon Road
historicsantafe.com/popelzaguan.html

This architectural gem was built in 1849 by James Johnson and features an unusual garden west of the house. Designed by Adolph Bandelier (Bandelier National Monument is named for him) in a formal Victorian style, the house has a garden boasting 100-year-old peony bushes and two large chestnut trees. The house itself grew over the years, including the addition of a covered passageway, or *zaguan*, from which addition the house derived its name. The house is now owned by the Historic Santa Fe Foundation, and its interior has been converted into rental apartments.

Olive Rush Studio
630 Canyon Road
collectorsguide.com/sf/sffa04.shtml

Olive Rush, who arrived in 1920, was one of the first female artists to live in Santa Fe. Little is known about the age of this house, but it is estimated that it was built in the early 1800s. Because Olive was a Quaker (the Society of Friends) the house was deeded to them and is lovingly maintained to this day.

Rafael Borrego House
724 Canyon Road
geronimorestaurant.com

Part of this very old house can be traced back to 1753 and reveals that it was typical of upscale homes of that era. Over the years rooms and refinements were added, including the Territorial *portal* now used by Geronimo restaurant for outdoor dining in the summer months. The restaurant is named after Geronimo Lopez, one of the house's first owners.

Cristo Rey Catholic Church. Built in 1940 by the parishioners, using about 200,000 adobe bricks that they fashioned by hand.

Cristo Rey Catholic Church
Canyon Road at Camino Cabra
(505) 983-8528
santafe.com/attractions/cristo_rey.html

This relatively new adobe church was built in 1940 to commemorate the 400th anniversary of Coronado's presence in New Mexico. Congregation members made the adobe bricks, about 200,000 of them, and helped to build the church. John Gaw Meem, an outstanding Santa Fe architect, designed it in the Spanish Mission style. One stunning feature of the church is the stone altar screen, originally carved in 1760 for the military chapel, La Castrense, located opposite the Palace of the Governors on the Plaza. The main saint depicted is Santiago—St. James—the patron saint of Spain.

- Open 8 a.m.-7 p.m. daily, free admission
- For information about the architecture, visit spanishcolonial. org/johngawmeem.html

5 MUSEUMS

Imagine a city of about 70,000 people with fourteen museums! That's probably a record of sorts, and there's good reason for this number. Santa Fe is both a historic city and an art community that draws from three cultures contributing to its unique creative style. Four state-run museums make up the Museum of New Mexico system: New Mexico Museum of Art, Palace of the Governors, Museum of Indian Arts and Culture and the Museum of International Folk Art.

museumofnewmexico.org
- shopmuseum.com

DOWNTOWN

In or near the Plaza area you'll find five museums to enjoy, each emphasizing both history and art.

Above: Georgia O'Keeffe Museum. A unique small museum devoted to the artwork of a unique woman.

Archdiocese of Santa Fe Museum
223 Cathedral Place
(505) 983-3811
collectorsguide.com/sf/sffa11.shtml

After touring the St. Francis Cathedral itself and viewing its collection of religious artifacts, you'll find a small museum that those interested in Santa Fe history will find appealing. Among the exhibits are Archbishop Lamy's boar hair trunk, the golden chalice given to him by Pope Pius IX in 1854 and a relic of the "True Cross."
- Open Monday-Friday, 9 a.m.-4 p.m.
- Donation requested.

Georgia O'Keeffe Museum
217 Johnson Street
(505) 995-0785
okeeffemuseum.org

The Georgia O'Keeffe Museum is the only museum in Santa Fe devoted to a single woman artist. Located in a small building remodeled from an old church, the museum presents a spare, indeed Spartan ambiance that helps to illuminate the artist and her work. This private museum opened in 1997 and is well worth a visit. The museum contains nine galleries, some showing O'Keeffe's work only, and some her work combined with that of her contemporaries from other collections to demonstrate the significance of her achievement within the history of modern American art.
- Open 10 a.m.-5 p.m. daily.
- Adults $8, seniors $7, New Mexico residents (with ID) $4.
- 5 p.m.-8 p.m. on Fridays only, free.

Institute of American Indian Arts Museum
108 Cathedral Place
(505) 983-8900
iaiancad.org

This museum of contemporary Indian arts opened in 1992. The former Federal Building (the post office) was renovated to create a venue for

Institute of American Indian Arts Museum showcases the work
of its students as well as established contemporary masters.

Indian artists from not only the Southwest but all over the country. A sculpture garden in the back features the work of renowned Chiricahua Apache sculptor Allan Houser.

- June-September: Monday-Saturday, 9 a.m.-5 p.m.; Sunday, 10 a.m.-5 p.m.
- October-May: Monday-Saturday, 10 a.m.-5 p.m.; Sunday, noon-5 p.m.
- Adults $4, seniors (62 and over) $2, students $2, children under 16 and members free.

New Mexico Museum of Art
107 West Palace Avenue
(505) 476-5072
24-hour recorded information: (505) 827-6463

nmartmuseum.org

This venerable art museum was founded in 1917. The museum's permanent collection of Santa Fe and Taos painters includes work by Georgia O'Keeffe, John Sloan and Ernest Blumenschein. Additionally, several exhibits each year feature the cutting edge of contemporary painting. Free tours with a docent are available.

- Open Tuesday-Sunday, 10 a.m.-5 p.m.
- $9 per person for one visit, one museum, one day only.
- $20 four-day pass, unlimited visits, all four New Mexico state museums.

- New Mexico residents $5, free all day Sunday.
- New Mexico senior citizens also free on Wednesdays.
- Children 16 and younger, always free.
- Friday 5 p.m.-8 p.m. free.

New Mexico History Museum
(incorporating the Palace of the Governors)
120 Lincoln Avenue
(505) 476-5100
24-hour recorded information: (505) 827-6463
palaceofthegovernors.org

Built between 1609 and 1610, the Palace of the Governors is the oldest continuously used government building in the United States. In 1912, it became the History Museum of New Mexico. Inside you will find Spanish and Indian artifacts, a portrait gallery of those who shaped Santa Fe, a chapel, and a courtyard. In 2009, a new contemporary wing was added to include the history of New Mexico and some of the treasures languishing in the basement. Free tours with a docent are available and offer an overview of New Mexico history from ancient times to the present.

- Open Tuesday-Sunday, 10 a.m.-5 p.m.
- $9 per person for one visit, one museum, one day only.
- $20 four-day pass, unlimited visits, all four New Mexico state museums.
- New Mexico residents: $5, free all day Sunday.
- New Mexico senior citizens also free on Wednesdays.
- Children 16 and younger, always free.
- Friday 5 p.m.-8 p.m. free.

JUST OFF THE PLAZA

Santuario de Guadalupe
100 South Guadalupe Street
(505) 988-2027
santafe.com/attractions/santuario_de_guadalupe.html

Just a short distance from the plaza is the historic Nuestra Señora de Guadalupe Church, the nation's oldest existing shrine to the Virgin of

Guadalupe. Restored in 2006, it is now an active church in the Archdiocese. Built in 1781, the Santuario houses the Archdiocese of Santa Fe's collection of New Mexican *santos* (carved images of the saints), Italian Renaissance paintings, and Mexican baroque paintings. Among the treasured works is Our Lady of Guadalupe, one of the largest and finest oil paintings of the Spanish Southwest, dated 1783 and signed by José de Alzibar, one of Mexico's most renowned painters.

Santuario de Guadalupe. The Virgin of Guadalupe statue conceived in Mexico and joyously installed in front of the church in 2008.

Indian Arts Research Center
At the School for Advanced Research on the
Human Experience
660 Garcia Street
(505) 954-7205
sarweb.org
sarweb.org/iarc/tours.htm

The School for Advanced Research on the Human Experience is little known by most tourists but is an absolute treasure source for collectors, researchers and scholars. It houses one of the most significant collections of traditional Southwest Indian arts and artifacts, spanning the 450-year period from Spanish contact to the present. Complemented by beautiful landscaping, this Spanish Pueblo Revival style building was once the home of newspaper heiress Amelia White, who bequeathed it to the school in 1972. Its collection of 11,000 artifacts includes pottery, textiles, paintings, basketry, jewelry and ethnographic materials.

- This collection is only open for viewing on Fridays at 2 p.m. with a docent-guided tour. $15 per person, advance reservations only.

MUSEUM HILL

Drive south on Old Santa Fe Trail, being sure you stay to the left when the road forks. About 1-1/2 miles from the Plaza you will come to Camino Lejo. Make a right and you'll be in the museum cluster. After parking, you will enter the Milner Plaza (completed in 2001), which leads to three of the museums.

- museumhill.org

Should you not have a car, you can take the "M" bus, which leaves Sheridan Street (one block over from the New Mexico Museum of Art). This bus starts running at 10 a.m. and every 45 minutes thereafter until 4:45 p.m. (Remember museums close at 5 p.m.) The bus leaves Museum Hill every 45 minutes beginning at 10:20 a.m. until 5:15 p.m.. The ride is approximately 18 minutes, and bus schedules are posted on the bus stops and online.

- santafetrails.santafenm.gov

Museum of Indian Arts and Culture
The Laboratory of Anthropology
710 Camino Lejo
(505) 476-1250
24-hour recorded information: (505) 827-6463
miaclab.org

Across the Milner Plaza is a museum built in 1986 to display artifacts

Museum of Indian Arts and Culture. A veritable treasure trove of Native American culture.

from Native American cultures. Housing over 50,000 pieces of textiles, clothing, pottery and basketry, it is a treasure trove of the ancient Southwest. Free tours with a docent are available.

- Open Tuesday-Sunday, 10 a.m.-5 p.m.
- $9 per person for one visit, one museum, one day only.
- $20 four-day pass, unlimited visits, all four New Mexico state museums.
- New Mexico residents $5, free all day Sunday.
- New Mexico senior citizens also free on Wednesdays.
- Children 16 and younger, always free.

Museum of International Folk Art
706 Camino Lejo
(505) 476-1200
24-hour recorded information: (505) 827-6463
moifa.org

This is one of the most unique museums in the country. Founded in 1953 by Florence Dibell Bartlett to show off her folk art collection, the museum enjoyed a significant increase in prestige with the acquisition in the 1980s of the Alexander Girard collection. Mr. Girard was a designer who loved primitive folk art, and his collection is an exquisite tribute to that genre. Young and old alike will love this fanciful section of the museum. In 1989, the Hispanic Heritage Wing was added to focus on folk art of the Southwest. Additionally, in 1999, Lloyd Cotzen donated the funds to build the Neutrogena Wing to house his collection of 5,000 artifacts and textiles from around the world, with items shown on a revolving basis. Free tours with a docent are available.

- Open Tuesday-Sunday, 10 a.m.-5 p.m.
- $9 per person for one visit, one museum, one day only.
- $20 four-day pass, unlimited visits, all four New Mexico state museums.
- New Mexico residents $5, free all day Sunday.
- New Mexico senior citizens also free on Wednesdays.
- Children 16 and younger, always free.

Over: Apache Mountain Spirit Dancer.
This statue dominates Milner Plaza, home to three museums.

Wheelwright Museum of the American Indian
704 Camino Lejo
(505) 982-4636
wheelwright.org

- Open Monday-Saturday, 10 a.m.-5 p.m., Sunday, 1 p.m.-5 p.m.
- Free admission.

Near the museum cluster run by the Museum of New Mexico Foundation is the private Wheelwright Museum. It was founded in 1937 by Mary Cabot Wheelwright and Navajo medicine man Hosteen Klah (1867-1937). A small gem of a museum, it's eight-sided, shaped like a hogan, or traditional Navajo home. Seasonally changing exhibitions in the main gallery include contemporary and traditional American Indian art, with an emphasis on the Southwest.

Museum of Spanish Colonial Arts
750 Camino Lejo
(505) 982-2226
spanishcolonial.org

Heading back on Camino Lejo to the Old Santa Fe Trail, consider

Museum of Spanish Colonial Art. Originally built as a private residence by renowned architect John Gaw Meem.

making your last stop the newest museum in Santa Fe. Opened in July of 2002, this compact, unique museum is built around a John Gaw Meem home and houses a collection of Spanish colonial furniture as well as art and artifacts including straw appliqué, pottery, wooden furniture, tinwork, and of course, carved saints (santos in Spanish). The collection spans the Middle Ages to the present. Free tours with a docent are available.

- Open Tuesday-Sunday, 10 a.m.-5 p.m.
- Adults $6, children 17 and under free, New Mexico residents $3.

Museum Hill Café
710 Camino Lejo
(505) 820-1776

museumhill.org/dine.php

This convenient and lovely café always has a selection of sandwiches, salads, desserts and drinks. A worthwhile stop after several hours in the museums.

- Tuesday through Saturday, 9 a.m.-3 p.m.
- Luncheon (and Sunday brunch), 11 a.m.-3 p.m.

"End of the Trail" statue at the entrance to Museum Hill depicts wagons coming from Missouri on the Santa Fe Trail.

FOR THE LATEST IN CONTEMPORARY ART

SITE Santa Fe
1606 Paseo de Peralta
(505) 989-1199
sitesantafe.org

Founded in 1993, SITE Santa Fe is a contemporary art museum and now part of the Railyard and Park. In their own words, the founders are "committed to the presentation of international, contemporary arts projects on a biennial basis." SITE Santa Fe is quite unusual and very intriguing—a must-see for those who like the avant-garde.
- Open Wednesday-Sunday, 10 a.m.-5 p.m.
- Friday, 10 a.m.-7 p.m.
- Adults $5, seniors and students $2.50, Friday free for everyone.

FOR THE YOUNG AND YOUNG AT HEART

El Rancho de Las Golondrinas
334 Las Pinos Road
(505) 471-2261
golondrinas.org

This "ranch of the swallows" goes back to the early 1700s and used to be a stopping place on the famous *Camino Real*, or "Royal Road," from Mexico City to Santa Fe. Opened as a "living-history" museum in 1972, it contains restored, authentic structures erected on old foundations. In this living history museum, villagers clothed in the styles of the times show how life was lived in early New Mexico. Attractions and celebrations abound, including harvest, wine and summer festivals, sheep shearing, horsemanship and a Civil War weekend, when visitors can see the villagers involved in day-to-day aspects of these events as well as in special reenactments. The Museum Shop at El Rancho de Las Golondrinas offers a fascinating collection of artwork and crafts in the tradition of early New Mexico. Call for information and directions from Santa Fe.
- Self-Guided Tours.
- June-September: Wednesday to Sunday, 10 a.m.-4 p.m.
- Adults $5, children (ages 5-12) $2.

- Seniors (62+), teens (ages 13-18), military personnel $4.
- Festival & Theme Weekend Admission Fees:
- Adults $7, Children (ages 5-12) $3.
- Seniors (62+), teens (ages 13-18), military personnel $5.
- Wine Festival Admission Fees:
- 21 and over $12, ages 13-20 $4.
- Josefina at Las Golondrinas™ Tours:
- Adults $10, children $7.
- Tours open to children ages 7 through 12 and their parents.
- Includes video and all-day admission to the museum. Reservations required.

Santa Fe Children's Museum

1050 Old Pecos Trail
(505) 989-8359
santafechildrensmuseum.org

If you're visiting with children, especially those under 12, we have a welcome diversion for all of you. The Children's Museum is a "hands on" activity place that involves magnets, live snakes, water, bubbles you can stand inside, weaving looms, even a climbing wall and much more. This is a respite from touring that your kids will treasure. Call for special events and times for toddlers.

- Open Wednesday-Saturday, 10 a.m.-5 p.m., Sunday, noon-5 p.m.
- Adults and children $8, New Mexico residents $4, Sundays for New Mexico residents $1.
- Children under 12 must be accompanied by an adult.

Stringing ristras at Las Golondrinas.
(Photo by George Locke, Las Golondrinas)

RESTAURANTS WITH A PAST

Rather than just recommend a restaurant for its cuisine alone, we have added a major ingredient—history—that we hope will double our dining pleasure. We've selected restaurants that not only have wonderful food but, also, many are located in historic buildings. After all, Santa Fe is a centuries-old city, so why not pick the places that bring the romance of the ages to your experience?

To learn more about these restaurants, or if you wish to search websites for most of Santa Fe's restaurants, log on to these websites:

- Visit santaferestaurants.net for capsule descriptions of almost every restaurant in town; easy to use and very helpful.
- Price Codes:
  $ inexpensive: up to $20
  $$ moderate: $20 to $35
  $$$ expensive: $35 to $55
  $$$$ very expensive: $55 or more

Above: Guadalupe Café. Enjoy a meal on the patio that fronts on Old Santa Fe Trail.

Amavi (formerly Julian's)
221 Shelby Street
(505) 988-2355
amavirestaurant.com

Julian's was always a local favorite and was voted Santa Fe's most romantic restaurant by both the *New Mexican* and the *Santa Fe Reporter* every year since 1998. The food is rustic Italian, French and Spanish regional cooking. As for its location, in Santa Fe terms, this lovely adobe building is not that old, only going back to the 1930s. But the feeling of the small rooms and *kiva* fireplaces adds an intimacy that you should experience.
* Serving dinner, $$$

Anasazi Restaurant
Inn of the Anasazi, 113 Washington Avenue
(505) 988-3030
innoftheanasazi.com/dine1.cfm

The Anasazi Restaurant, one of Santa Fe's most highly acclaimed eateries, features contemporary Southwestern cuisine, including Native American, Northern New Mexican and Southwestern. Chefs take advantage of New Mexico's abundance of fresh fruits and vegetables, as well as organic meats and poultry. The ambience is extraordinary, as the architects incorporated influences from the ancient Anasazi peoples as well as more modern arts and crafts from New Mexico's three cultures—Native American, Hispanic and Anglo. The Inn, built in 1991, was constructed on the site of the State Securities Building, whose white pillars reminded one of New England.
* Serving breakfast, lunch and dinner, $$$-$$$$

Bull Ring
150 Washington Avenue
(505) 983-3328
santafebullring.com

Although no longer located in a 150-year-old adobe building, the Bull Ring has its own historical significance—as the most popular dining and gathering spot for state and local political figures. Primarily a steakhouse and lounge, the Bull Ring is also a place where Santa Feans know they can run into friends and share good times.

• Serving lunch and dinner, $$$

Café Pasqual's
121 Don Gaspar Avenue
(800) 722-7672 or
(505) 983-9340
pasquals.com

Although not housed in a truly historic building (circa 1920s), this venerable 30-year-old restaurant is a keeper. Always mobbed and festive, it displays murals by Oaxacan artist Leovigildo Martinez. It embodies Northern New Mexican, Old Mexican and Asian culinary traditions, served in Santa Fe style. Winner of the 1999 James Beard American Regional Cooking Classics award, Pasqual's uses only fresh, seasonal, organic and naturally raised foods.

Left: Café Pasqual's, a favorite among locals and tourists alike.

• Serving breakfast, lunch and dinner, $$-$$$

Coyote Café
132 West Water Street
(505) 983-1615
coyotecafe.com/santafe.htm

Eric DiStefano's Coyote Café, without question, is one of Santa Fe's most famous restaurants and was voted most popular by Zagat Guide. The dazzlingly creative blend of flavors based on the traditional cuisines of the Southwest. As for its location, believe it or not, this building was once the Santa Fe Bus Depot! The remodeling of this place still retains delightful touches of times gone by. For example, the serving area adjacent to the open kitchen was once the ticket counter.

- Coyote Café: serving dinner and weekend brunch, $$$$
- Rooftop Cantina: serving lunch and dinner, warm months, $$-$$$

Fuego at La Posada
330 East Palace Avenue
(505) 954-9670
laposada.rockresorts.com/info/din.fuego.asp

This beautifully appointed restaurant is located within the luxurious La Posada de Santa Fe, inside part of the original building erected in 1882 by Abraham Staab, one of the city's most prominent German Jewish merchants. Local folklore tells us that Julia Schuster Staab, the merchant's wife, suffered from severe postpartum depression and died in 1896. Her ghost now haunts the old part of the hotel and presents herself in the bar, in the library and on the staircase near her room. She has been known to pull covers from the bed at night in the upstairs bedroom where she died. Ask hotel personnel at the main desk to show you Julia Staab's room, No. 100—if it isn't occupied by the living!

In modern times, Fuego invites you to enjoy roaring wood fires from comfortable leather couches during the winter. In summer, listen to the whisper of the breezes on the outdoor patio. Fuego serves outstanding traditional and contemporary dishes infused with regional ingredients and flavors, often accompanied by melodic tones of a flamenco guitar.

- Serving breakfast, lunch and dinner, $$$-$$$$

Guadalupe Café
422 Old Santa Fe Trail
(505) 982-9762

Guadalupe Café, an institution in Santa Fe for 40 years, is best known for its wonderful, expansive breakfast menu. Also serving lunch and dinner, the restaurant features New Mexican cooking, in portions that are ample, to say the least. Its simple adobe building, composed of several small rooms, dates to the late 1800s, when it was a private residence.

After your meal, wander through the art galleries of the State Capitol, right next door.

• Serving breakfast, lunch and dinner, $-$$

La Casa Sena
Sena Plaza, 125 East Palace Avenue
(505) 988-9232
lacasasena.com

In summer, the courtyard of La Casa Sena provides a romantic setting for drinks or a sublime dining experience. The menu features innovative Southwestern cuisine and a fabulous wine list. For a more casual dining experience, visit La Cantina, where you will be entertained by Santa Fe's only singing waiters, who perform jazz and Broadway revues nightly.

As for the location, the 1796 Sena hacienda is both charming and authentic. Jose Sena, a Mexican Army Major, lived in this dwelling with his wife and children. In the original hacienda, all the windows were placed inside looking out on the inner courtyard; there weren't any outside

The romantic, lush courtyard of La Casa Sena Restaurant.

windows then because of possible Indian attacks. Now, there are many shops and many windows! In the 1800s, the courtyard was a dusty place where livestock and chickens ran free; today, it is beautifully planted with stately old trees and seasonal flowers.

• Serving lunch and dinner every day, $$-$$$

La Plazuela at La Fonda
100 East San Francisco Street
(505) 982-5511
lafondasantafe.com/foodbev/foodbev.html

La Plazuela, a beautiful enclosed skylit courtyard restaurant in La Fonda lobby, is quite Spanish in feeling, and it's a great place to people-watch. The food, prepared by an award-winning culinary team, is Mexican and New Mexican in nature and is consistently good. Ernesto Martinez, a local artist, created the painted panes of glass depicting flowers and birds that run from the floor to the ceiling. As discussed, La Fonda itself is a much-storied place. Just being in the lobby evokes memories of times gone by. Every evening, the area just off the bar is reserved for country-western dancing.

• Serving breakfast, lunch and dinner, $$-$$$

The Old House
Located in the Eldorado Hotel
309 West San Francisco Street
(800) 286-6755 or (505) 988-4455
eldoradohotel.com/restaurants/oldhouse.htm

The Old House is the only Mobil four-star, AAA four-diamond restaurant in the state and Zagat's top choice for New Mexico dining. Its wine list has been honored by *Wine Spectator*. The restaurant features Southwestern cuisine tempered with a touch of continental, enhanced by innovative presentation and impeccable service in a cozy, yet elegant atmosphere. As for the location, the architects tried to construct the new restaurant inside an adobe house from the late 1700s located on the hotel property. Unfortunately, it was structurally unsound and had to be torn down. But the Old House is on the site of the old building (and named after it), so you'll have to imagine yourself eating in a 1700s house. With the restaurant's ambience, that shouldn't be hard to do.

- Serving dinner, $$$$

Pink Adobe
406 Old Santa Fe Trail
(505) 983-7712
thepinkadobe.com

Rosalea Murphy opened this famous restaurant in 1944. It features American/Creole and New Mexican specialties. In recent years, the Pink Adobe has become a gathering place for locals, visitors and famous personalities, including presidents, movie stars and some of the most interesting characters known to Santa Fe. Its Dragon Room bar is known the world over.

Watch the flickering candle at your table, close your eyes and for a moment you'll be transported back to the 18th century. Located in the historic Barrio de Analco neighborhood, the 300-year-old building itself

The Pink Adobe. Lunch and dinner are served in a most romantic setting.

was a military barracks during the Spanish occupation. The walls are three feet thick, and the restaurant is replete with fireplaces and artwork.

• Serving lunch and dinner, $$-$$$

Plaza Restaurant
54 Lincoln Avenue
(505) 982-1664

This time-honored standby—a local favorite—features some colorful neon signs and a long lunch counter, along with booths against the walls and a few tables. You can depend on the place for a good Northern New Mexico meal, the basic "American" breakfast and lunch dishes, as well as Greek and international foods. As for its history, the Plaza Restaurant rates a visit because it is the oldest restaurant (1905) in town. There are others in much older buildings, but any establishment that has survived over 100 years is worth looking into. Its early-20th-century decor reflects its beginnings.

• Serving breakfast, lunch and dinner, $-$$

Rio Chama Steakhouse
414 Old Santa Fe Trail
(505) 955-0765
riochamasteakhouse.com

Rio Chama Steakhouse, located right on Old Santa Fe Trail, spe-

cializes in steak and choice beef. Although it is a new restaurant, it has the look of a venerable Pueblo Revival building and has a beautiful outdoor patio. Rio Chama Steakhouse serves the

Rio Chama Steakhouse. Good food in a wonderful setting amid Western artwork.

finest prime and choice dry aged steaks, chops and seafood. Located in the historic Barrio de Analco neighborhood, this building once housed another steak restaurant and before that, a private residence in the 1850s. Many of the original adobe walls were retained as the modern restaurant evolved.

• Serving lunch and dinner, $$$-$$$$

Santacafé
231 Washington Avenue
(505) 984-1788
santacafe.com

Although the menu changes seasonally, Santacafé's American offerings are always intertwined with touches of Northern New Mexican spice. The patio opens in the late spring for outdoor dining. This elegant restaurant offers artistically presented, creative dishes and a caring, attentive staff. As for its history, Santacafé is located inside the Padre Gallegos House, built between 1827 and 1862. Señor José M. Gallegos was a colorful priest and a politician—quite a combination! Unfortunately, his outspoken ways led to his being defrocked by Archbishop Lamy in 1852. He then entered politics and was the delegate from the New Mexico Territory from 1853 to 1855 and from 1871 to 1873. Born in 1815, he died in 1875 and is buried in Santa Fe's Rosario Cemetery.

• Serving lunch and dinner, $$-$$$

The Shed
113-1/2 East Palace Avenue
(505) 982-9030
sfshed.com

Often visitors have heard about this place before they get to town—it's been a very "Santa Fe" spot for lunch or dinner since 1953, and its chile dishes are world renowned. Typically Northern New Mexican, one featured dish is blue corn enchiladas with red chile and garlic bread and another is the pollo adobo, chicken roasted in red adobo marinade, garlic and oregano. If you can, finish up with one of the delectable desserts. As for the location, this historic adobe hacienda, dating to 1692, was originally the home of Antonine Roubidoux, a French fur trapper and then the home of Bradford Prince, one of New Mexico's Territorial governors. Prince purchased the home in 1879 and lived there with his wife for forty years. A room designed by Mrs. Prince in the Victorian style can be seen at the Palace of the Governors. The Shed also owns another restaurant, La Choza.

- Serving lunch and dinner, $-$$

Nostrani (formerly Rociada)
304 Johnson Street
(505) 983-3800
nostrani.com

This is the only Santa Fe restaurant to make *Gourmet* magazine's Top 50 in 2006. The atmosphere and the food complement each other. Specializing in Northern Italian cuisine with the most comprehensive wine list in New Mexico, Nostrani offers dishes like veal scaloppine with Tuscan vegetable ragú and orzo. The seasonal menu offers the freshest and finest ingredients available. Enjoy patio dining from May through October. As for the location, the building dates from 1857. Recently renovated, it reminds one of an old farmhouse placed in a trendy SoHo setting. The renovation has preserved the architectural integrity of the gracefully flowing interior with handsome turn-of-the-century tin ceilings and adobe archways.

- Serving dinner, $$$-$$$$

Nostrani. Enjoy gourmet food in a beautifully restored 1857 house.

Upper Crust Pizza
329 Old Santa Fe Trail
(505) 982-0000, free delivery
uppercrustpizza.com

This pizza restaurant, consistently voted "Best of Santa Fe," has been around since 1979. In addition to the traditional pizzas, Upper Crust creates some in Santa Fe style with green chile or Mexican sausage, with whole-wheat or traditional Italian crusts. It also serves great sandwiches, calzones and salads. You can enjoy the Santa Fe scene from the large front patio, or, if you prefer, you can have your pizza delivered to your room. Strange place for a pizza parlor to be, but this building is part of the Barrio de Analco.

- Serving lunch and dinner, $

CANYON ROAD

The Compound
653 Canyon Road
(505) 982-4353
compoundrestaurant.com

If the weather is warm and sunny (your chances are very good), opt for lunch or dinner on the garden patio. Contemporary American food reigns here, and it is excellent, paired with a thoughtful selection of wine and classical service in a relaxed atmosphere. Attention to detail and professional service complement the dining experience. As for the location, this house was built around 1850 with small dining rooms that spill out onto the gorgeous enclosed patio. Before its incarnation as a restaurant, The Compound was the centerpiece of a group of houses on Canyon Road known as the McComb Compound. In the earlier part of the 20th century, when Santa Fe was a long way from the rest of the world, movie stars, industrialists and socialites visited, where they could rent a house in relative seclusion. Alexander Girard, whose collections of folk art grace the Museum of International Folk Art, decorated the original restaurant. Some of his touches are still to be seen in the updated Compound. Chef Mark Kiffin won the James Beard Chef of the Southwest Award in 2006.

- Serving lunch and dinner, $$$$

El Farol
808 Canyon Road
(505) 983-9912
elfarolsf.com

Santa Fe's oldest restaurant and cantina, El Farol is a local favorite for both its excellent food and superb entertainment. The restaurant serves award-winning traditional and contemporary Spanish cuisine, featuring over 35 different tapas—small, delectable Spanish dishes or appetizers. You can mix or match these delectable treats to create a meal or order a more traditional dinner. The famous and infamous can show up here— good people-watching! Owner David Salazar invites you to come and enjoy the finest live entertainment in Santa Fe, including jazz, soul, folk, R&B and flamenco, every night of the week.

As for its location, El Farol is housed in an adobe building that has served artists, locals and stray bohemians since 1835. If they could talk, these thick old walls would tell stories of lovers, poets, musicians and artists, like painter Alfred Morang, whose frescoes adorn them. These were painted between 1945 and 1952, when the cantina still had dirt floors. The decor is a cross between rustic Spanish and rustic Santa Fe.

- Serving lunch and dinner, $$-$$$

El Farol. Santa Fe's oldest restaurant and cantina is a favorite for both its excellent food and entertainment.

Geronimo
724 Canyon Road
(505) 982-1500

After 18 celebrated years, Geronimo has established a reputation as the place to dine in Santa Fe. It has succeeded in bringing unparalleled sophistication with a romantic, elegant atmosphere, creating a fabulous backdrop for the contemporary American-Southwest and Far East influenced creations. Appetizers, salads and desserts along with seafood and meat dishes alike are wonderfully prepared in this romantic spot. The building is over 250 years old, and the interior is reflective of that period in a sparse, elegant way. This 1756 landmark adobe was built by Geronimo Lopez.

- geronimorestaurant.com/
- Serving lunch and dinner, $$$-$$$$

GUADALUPE DISTRICT and AGUA FRÍA STREET

Azur Mediterranean Kitchen
428 Aqua Fria
(505) 992-2897
azursantafe.com

The younger sister of acclaimed restaurant Ristra, Azur recently

Geronimo. Enjoy fabulous food while dining in an over-250-year-old building.

opened serving such dishes as Moroccan tangines, mahi mahi with green olive, raisins, capers, served on a herbed couscous and wide selection of tapas. Wines from France, Italy and Spain, of course.
  • Serving lunch and dinner $$-$$$

Café Café
500 Sandoval Street
(505) 995-9595

Basically Italian, this sophisticated but low-key eatery was named 2008 Restaurant of the Year by the *Santa Fe Reporter*. From pizza to Tuscan clam chowder to the coffee and chile rubbed beef tenderloin you won't be disappointed.
  • Lunch and dinner, $$

Clafoutis
402 North Guadalupe Street
(505) 988-1809

Since Clafoutis opened a short time ago, the restaurant has been packed. And with good reason. Pastries to die for, croissants and baguettes as good as the ones Parisians eat, along with omelettes, salads, crêpes, all priced right, make this a special place run by a very special French couple.
  • Breakfast and lunch, Monday-Saturday, $

Cowgirl Bar & Grill
319 South Guadalupe Street
(505) 982-2565
(cowgirl-santafe.com/

Specializing in mesquite-smoked pit barbeque, as well as steaks, chicken and New Mexican favorites, with nightly live entertainment. American and imported beers a specialty.
  • Serving lunch and dinner, with Saturday and Sunday breakfasts, $$

Paddy Rawal's Raaga Fine Indian Dining
544 Aqua Fria
505 820-6440
Raagacuisine.com

Santa Fe is not all about tamales and chile. Enter Paddy Rawal who electic brand of food from India offers an abundance vegetarian fare plus shrimp, chicken and fish dishes with a decided India kick. Of course, the dishes we all love like vindaloos and tandori accompanied with naan are mainstays of the menu. Not to be missed.
- Serving lunch and dinner and delivery daily $$-$$$

Ristra
548 Agua Fría Street
(505) 982-8608
ristrarestaurant.com

Ristra offers an eclectic blend of Southwestern and French cuisine. The intimate surroundings are warm and casual, yet elegant. Weather permitting, you can dine on the lovely outdoor patio. As for its location, this building is unlike most of the classic adobe and Territorial buildings that make up much of Santa Fe. It's an old bungalow-style cottage, probably built after 1880 when the railroad came through and bricks became more plentiful. As you walk through the small dining room areas, however, the interior has an indigenous adobe feel.
- Serving dinner, $$$$

Tomasita's Santa Fe Station
500 South Guadalupe Street
(505) 983-5721

Always a popular place because of its Northern New Mexican cooking and its moderate prices, Tomasita's is always crowded. No reservations are accepted, so be prepared to wait—but you can get a drink from the bar and the wait is worth it! The frozen margaritas are a hallmark of the restaurant, as are such dishes as chile rellenos and blue corn chicken enchiladas. The building once housed a brick trackside warehouse for the

"Chile Line," a spur railroad that ran from 1884 to 1941. In its day, it was the "lifeline" to Northern New Mexico towns and pueblos.
- Serving lunch and dinner daily, $-$$

SANTA FE'S BEST-KEPT SECRETS

The following restaurants are favorites with locals and always packed. Some do not take reservations, but all are worth the wait. They are in general more casual and less expensive.

315
315 Old Santa Fe Trail
(505) 986-9190
315santafe.com

A lovely old building on historic Old Santa Fe Trail houses this restaurant reminiscent of a French Country Inn. Seared Duckling in Potato Galette is not to be missed. Includes a wine bar.
- Serving lunch and dinner $$-$$$

Andiamo
322 Garfield Street
(505) 995-9595
andiamoonline.com

One of the premier Italian restaurants in town, Andiamo is a must for its food and ambience. Try the Baked Risotto with Mushroom Ragout.
- Serving lunch and dinner $$

Aqua Santa
457 West Alameda Street
(505) 982-6297

Be assured that the host and owner will greet you like you are a local; this place reverberates warmth and charm. Homemade bread, Breast of Guinea Hen and mussels are all excellent.
- Serving lunch and dinner $$$

Blue Corn Café

133 Water Street (just off the Plaza)
(505) 984-1800
4056 Cerrillos Road (near Santa Fe Place Mall)
(505) 438-1800
bluecorncafe.com

Enjoy locally brewed beer and ale along with a variety of Northern New Mexico specialties.
- Serving lunch and dinner, $-$$

Bobcat Bite

420 Old Las Vegas Highway
(505) 983-5319, call for directions
bobcatbite.com

Since 1953 this diner-style restaurant has been turning out the best inch-and-one-half-hamburgers and green chile cheeseburgers in Santa Fe. Filmmakers have incorporated it into their documentaries. *Gourmet* magazine has featured this five-table, nine-counter-seat unique restaurant. Be prepared to wait a bit for a chair. Cash only.
- Serving lunch and dinner Wednesday through Saturday, $

Counter Culture

930 Baca Street
(505) 995-1105

Off the beaten path, this locals' place serves sophisticated food in a no-frills environment. Jason excels in healthy large salads, mussels, grilled salmon with leeks in a Pernod cream sauce and a sensational hanger steak. Cash and local checks only.
- Serving breakfast, lunch and dinner, $

El Mesón Restaurant Tapas Bar

213 Washington Avenue
(505) 983-6756
elmeson-santafe.com

If you'd like to be eating in a restaurant in Spain then head over to El

Mesón, Santa Fe's equivalent. Not only will you be ordering tapas and paellas, but you'll do it to the rhythms of Spanish guitar or Argentine tango music. The owner and chef David Huertas delivers the goods.
- Serving dinner Tuesday-Saturday, $$-$$$

Harry's Roadhouse
96-B Old Las Vegas Highway
(505) 989-4629

A local favorite, Harry's menu features a wide variety of foods with something to please any taste, all of it fresh and homemade.
- Serving breakfast, lunch and dinner, $-$$

Il Piatto
95 West Marcy Street
(505) 984-1091

An Italian perennial on Marcy Street, many locals dine here. My absolute favorite is the Lemon and Rosemary Grilled Chicken.
- Serving lunch and dinner, $$-$$$

Jambo Café
2010 Cerrillos Road (located in a shopping
center off of Cerrillos and St. Michaels)
(505) 473-1269

Have you had your fill of tamales and chile rellenos? Jambo introduces you to African-Caribbean food that you'll long remember. Goat stew, Moroccan lamb stew, delicious peanut inspired soups and a curried chicken salad wrap are a few of our favorite things.
- Serving lunch and dinner $$

Kakawa Chocolate House
1050 Paseo de Peralta
(505) 982-0388
kakawachocolates.com

Just across from the Gerald Peters Gallery, hidden from view is Kakawa, a most unusual place specializing in Mesoamerican Chocolate Elixers. They're made from bittersweet chocolate with historic recipes from 2000

BC from Central America a Mexico. Intriguing? Additionally, they have a flourless chocolate torte and passionate dark chocolate candies. All this in a 1938 adobe house. Mmm . . .

La Boca
72 West Marcy Street
(505) 982-3433

James Campbell Caruso, who wrote a definitive book on tapas, presides over this restaurant specializing in tapas (of course), *bocadillos* and other dishes from Spain.
- Serving lunch, tapas and dinner, $$-$$$

La Choza
905 Alarid Street
(505) 982-0909

Specializing in Northern New Mexican food since 1984, La Choza is situated in an old adobe that served as the ranch house and bunkhouse for the Mercer Ranch in the early 1900s. Owned and operated by The Shed Restaurant, La Choza is a favorite with locals who come to savor the sopaipillas, chalupas, tamales and carne adovada.
- Serving lunch and dinner, $-$$

Maria's New Mexican Kitchen
555 West Cordova Road
(505) 983-7929
marias-santafe.com

Maria's is known for margaritas—over 100 are featured—as well as for its *fajitas*. Enjoy patio dining in the summer. The owner, Al Lucero, is the author of *The Great Margarita Book*.
- Serving lunch and dinner, $-$$

Mu Du Noodles
1494 Cerrillos Road
(505) 983-1411

Mu Jing Lau has run this pan-Asian restaurant since 1997 with an artistic innovative style all her own. Named 2010 Restaurant of the Year by

the *Santa Fe Reporter*, it is consistently excellent. Try the Sunday brunch Dim Sum for an unusual treat.
- Serving Dinner 5:30-9 p.m. Tuesday-Sunday and Sunday Brunch $$$

O'Keeffe Café
217 Johnson Street
(505) 946-1065
okeeffecafe.com

This contemporary Southwest restaurant with a French flair is right next door to the museum. It is housed in a 150-year-old Territorial that was a barracks for Union Officers in the mid-1800s.

O'Keeffe Café. After touring the O'Keeffe Museum, walk next door to the café for excellent food in a lovely setting.

- Serving lunch and dinner, $$$

Ore House at Milagro
139 West San Francisco
(505) 983-8687
orehouseatmilagro.com

Long a favorite of Santa Fe, the Ore House has combined with its sister restaurant Milagro 139 to continue to offer steak, seafood and New Mexico specialties. Open daily for drinks, appetizers and desserts. In their spacious courtyard you can sip on one of 40 different margaritas. The restaurant has been winning the Wine Spectator Award of Excellence since 1993.
- Open for lunch and dinner, $$$

Restaurant Martín
526 Galisteo Street
(505) 820-0919

Martín Rios, formerly head chef at The Old House, Anasazi and Geronimo's, opened his own place in 2009. It's been packed ever since. Try the Ahi Tuna or the grilled Berkshire pork chop and judge for yourself.
- Serving lunch, dinner and brunch, $$$

Santa Fe Baking Co. and Café
504 West Cordova Road
(505) 988-4292
santafebakingcompanycafe.com/

One of the area's favorite meeting places, especially for breakfast, coffee break and lunch. Bakery as well as full breakfast and lunch menus.
- Serving breakfast and lunch, $

Second Street Brewery
1814 Second Street and
1607 Paseo de Peralta (at the Railyard)
(505) 982-3030 and 989-3278
secondstreetbrewery.com

A neighborhood brewpub offering locally made English-style ales and authentic international pub food, frequently with live music.
- Serving appetizers, lunch and dinner, $-$$

Steaksmith
104-B Old Las Vegas Highway
(505) 988-3333
santafesteaksmith.com

Santa Fe's steak and seafood house since 1973 features choice aged beef, as well as an extensive appetizer and light meal menu in the lounge.
- Serving dinner, $$-$$$

The Tea House
821 Canyon Road
(505) 992-0972

A "find" at the top of Canyon Road, the Tea House offers soups, salads, sandwiches and of course an amazing selection of teas. You'll see many laptops in use and tea drinkers whiling away the day.
- Serving breakfast, lunch and dinner, $$

Tecolote Café
1203 Cerrillos Road
(505) 988-1362

Tourists and locals alike agree that this is the place to go for a great homemade breakfast. Large portions, lots of chile and friendly service.
- Serving breakfast and lunch until 2 p.m., $

Terra
The restaurant at Encantado, an Auberge resort,
just outside of Tesuque, call for directions.
(505) 988-9955
encandatoresort.com

Terra, recently opened in this Auberge Resort, is getting stellar reviews. Chef Charles Dale has designed a menu that features lobster tortilla soup, rack of lamb and even a duck tamale.
- Serving dinner, $$$$

Tesuque Village Market
Five miles north of Santa Fe in Tesuque,
call for directions
(505) 988-8848

Enjoy American and Southwestern specialties. Also sells groceries, pastries, deli items and liquor.
- Serving breakfast, lunch and dinner, $-$$

Tia Sophia's
210 West San Francisco Street
(505) 983-9880

This popular downtown restaurant is famous for its breakfast burritos. The menu has the following note: "Not responsible for too hot chile."
- Serving breakfast and lunch, $

Tune-up Café
1115 Hickox Street
(505) 983-7060

An interesting blend of Salvadoran, Mexican, Cuban and American foods make this casual newcomer a hit. Try the Salvadoran Pupasas or the incredible buffalo burger on a brioche bun. It has been on the Food Channel's "Diners, Drive-Ins and Dives."
- Serving breakfast, lunch and dinner, $$

Vinaigrette
709 Don Cubero Alley
(505) 820-9205

Salads of all kinds dominate this sleek restaurant. Owner Erin Wade owns a farm in Nambé, and in season all the produce comes from there. Try a most delectable Cobb salad. You can add beef, chicken, duck, pork, tuna or scallops to any of the salads.

• Serving lunch and dinner, $$

Zia Diner
326 South Guadalupe
(505) 988-7008
ziadiner.com

This upscale diner features daily specials of pasta, fish, chicken and diner comfort food.

• Serving lunch and dinner, $-$$

WHO AND WHAT'S COOKING?
(You are!)

Once you've been smitten by the flavors and aromas of Southwestern cooking, the next step is to take a cooking class in town. Here are two excellent choices:

Santa Fe School of Cooking
116 West San Francisco Street
(505) 983-4511
santafeschoolofcooking.com

The owners, a mother and daughter team, head up a staff of nine outstanding chefs who teach the secrets of regional cooking. Their hands-on tamale class is especially popular. Whatever you prepare you will enjoy for lunch. Check the website for their other culinary adventures.

Las Cosas
Kitchen Shoppe and Cooking School
DeVargas Center, 181 Paseo de Peralta
(505) 988-3394
lascosascooking.com

John Vollertsen, food columnist for the *Santa Fe New Mexican*, leads these eclectic cooking classes throughout the year. They include "New Mexico Favorites," "Unique Italian Cookery" and "Thai Soups and Stir Frys."

COOKING CLASSES MAY LEAD TO BUYING COOKBOOKS

Even if you don't take a cooking class in Santa Fe, you're apt to buy a cookbook or two to take home. Here are some of my favorites:

Southwest Flavors—Santa Fe School of Cooking by Susan Curtis and Nicole Curtis Ammerman. $34.95

The Big Book of Outdoor Cooking and Entertainment by Cheryl and Bill Jamison. $24.95

Culinary Mexico by Daniel Hoyer. $34.95

Café Pasqual's—Recipes from Santa Fe's Renowned Corner Café by Katherine Kagel. $22.95

Palette in the Kitchen (favorite recipes from New Mexico artists) compiled by Constance Counter and Karl Tani. $16.95

Vegetarian Cooking for Everyone by Deborah Madison. $40

The world renowned chef and writer, who lives in the Santa Fe area, was the founder of the famous Green's Restaurant in San Francisco.

Santa Fe Kitchens by the Museum of New Mexico. $29.95

Season of Santa Fe, a cookbook by Kitchen Angels of Santa Fe. $19.95

Cooking with Johnny Vee, by John Vollertsen, Las Cosas Cooking School. $24.95

LODGINGS WITH A PAST

Whenever I visit a historical town I want to feel its history and the romance, so I search for accommodations that go hand in glove with the roots of the place. Here is a list of Santa Fe lodgings for historical bedding-down. There are, of course, motels galore on Cerrillos Road and several beautiful but new upscale hotels in town, and you're welcome to check these out, but I recommend you go for the history and the home-made breakfasts.

- Price codes:
  - $$ $100-$150
  - $$$ over $150
  - $$$$ over $200

HISTORIC BED & BREAKFASTS

Adobe Abode Bed & Breakfast
202 Chapelle Street
(505) 983-3133, $$$
adobeabode.com

Located close to the Plaza, this 1907 adobe has rooms that reflect different styles and moods—Provence, perhaps, or Cowboy, or Mexican. Along with its Old World charm come amenities such as cushy robes and designer linens, along with cookies and sherry served all day.

Don Gaspar Inn
623 Don Gaspar Avenue
(888) 986-8664 or (505) 986-8664, $$$
dongaspar.com

Located in a historic neighborhood where many of the early merchants built their homes, this inn compound features three older buildings: a 1900-1910 arts-and-crafts brick bungalow, a 1910 Territorial building and a 1930s Pueblo-style building. All three have a Victorian interior-decorating theme. The ultimate garden features irises and lilies and more in a fountain setting that one would expect to see on the East Coast. Voted one of the Top Ten Romantic Inns in the Country for 2003 by *American Historic Inns*.

El Paradero Bed & Breakfast Inn
220 West Manhattan Avenue
(505) 988-1177, $$$
elparadero.com

Originally a Spanish farmhouse built between 1800 and 1820, this building was once far from "town." Now it's near the Sanbusco Market Center, the Farmers' Market and many restaurants. Pillars were added in the late 19th century, Victorian touches in 1912. Its current owners tried to keep the "adobe farmhouse feeling" intact, and they have succeeded. Some rooms are moderately priced; the more expensive ones have different furnishings and mountain views. Breakfasts are ample and feature a special entrée daily.

Four Kachinas Inn
512 Webber Street
(888) 634-8282 or (505) 988-1631, $$$
fourkachinas.com

Located on a quiet residential street in the Don Gaspar Historic District, the Four Kachinas Inn is a short block from the Plaza. One of the guest rooms is located in the historic Digneo House, built in 1910 by Carlo Digneo, one of the Italian stonemasons who completed the St. Francis Cathedral for Archbishop Lamy in the late 19th century. All the rooms feature quality Southwestern art and locally made crafts. In summer enjoy a delightful continental breakfast in the outside garden patio.

Guadalupe Inn
604 Agua Fría Street
(505) 989-7422, $$
guadalupeinn.com

Enjoy traditional Santa Fe family hospitality in this small inn, a "truly Santa Fe" experience. Owned and operated by three members of the Quintana family, the inn was built on the site of their grandfather's store on Agua Fría, very close to the historic Santuario de Guadalupe. Although the building itself is quite new, the land has been in the Quintana family for generations; in fact, Concha S. Quintana, now in her 90s, will regale you at breakfast with tale after tale of Santa Fe in the old days, when she used to work at La Fonda and met all the artists and celebrities. Some rooms have whirlpool tubs, fireplaces and mountain views. For breakfast, visitors select from a menu ranging from traditional New Mexico family favorites to eggs any style and pancakes.

Hacienda Nicholas
320 East Marcy Street
(888) 877-7622 or (505) 992-8385, $$-$$$
haciendanicholas.com

The Hacienda Nicholas, owned by Carolyn Lee and named for her son, is a beautifully understated adobe. In her words: "The decor throughout the house is an elegant blend of Southwest meets Provence." Legend has it that this beautiful adobe hacienda was built in 1910 by Antonio Abelard Rodriguez for his bride, the exquisite Doña Isabella. Breakfasts are substantial and include such entrées as blueberry pancakes, quiche and breakfast frittatas.

Inn of the Five Graces
(Formerly Seret's 1001 Nights)
150 East De Vargas Street
(866) 992-0957 or (505) 992-0957, $$$$
fivegraces.com

Inn of the Five Graces is located in the Barrio de Analco. The innkeepers have chosen to combine Santa Fe's Southwestern buildings with an alluring amalgamation of textiles and wooden pieces from Turkey, India, Tibet and Afghanistan, with a warm, romantic result. The years of construction of the buildings themselves ranges from 1888 to 1950. New Mexico river rock was used for one built in 1938. Recently acquired by the Garrett Hotel Group, Inn of the Five Graces is high on service and amenities. All units come with kitchens and elegant baths, and many have fireplaces.

Inn of the Turquoise Bear
342 Buena Vista Street
(800) 396-4104 or (505) 983-0798, $$$-$$$$
turquoisebear.com

This B&B dates to the mid-1800s and was once the home of poet Witter Bynner (1881-1968), a noted member of the cultural group flourishing at that time in Santa Fe. The bedrooms are simple but well appointed with flowers, fruits and complimentary robes; the public rooms are ranch-like and very appealing.

The inn's sense of history lies partly in who "partied" here. Mr. Bynner hosted many bashes with such notables as D. H. Lawrence, Ansel Adams, Igor Stravinsky, Willa Cather, Georgia O'Keeffe, Edna St. Vincent Millay, Robert Frost, Martha Graham, Rita Hayworth and Frida Kahlo. Oh, to be a fly on the wall at those soirées!

Pueblo Bonito Inn
138 West Manhattan Avenue
(800) 461-4599 or (505) 984-8001, $$$
pueblobonitoinn.com

Built in 1873, this old adobe edifice is but a short walk to the Plaza. Most of the furnishings are Southwestern—santos, paintings and pottery— and *kiva* fireplaces grace every one of the 15 rooms. A continental breakfast is served buffet style; later in the day, relax with afternoon tea.

HISTORIC HOTELS

Hilton of Santa Fe
100 Sandoval Street
(800) 336-3676 or (505) 988-2811, $$$-$$$$
hiltonofsantafe.com

Decorated throughout with beautiful regional artwork and antiquities, the Hilton of Santa Fe also preserves the historic Antonio Jose Ortiz Hacienda, built in the 1700s and one of Santa Fe's well-known historical sites. For restaurants you can select from the Piñon Grill, El Cañon and the Chamisa Courtyard Café.

The Hotel St. Francis
210 Don Gaspar Avenue
(800) 529-5700 or 983-5700, $$$$
hotelstfrancis.com

The Hotel St. Francis, recently renovated—listed in the National Register of Historic Places—is close to the Plaza, shopping and wonderful restaurants. Guest quarters embody a Victorian sensibility, with brass and iron beds and furniture of cherry wood and marble.

La Fonda
100 East San Francisco Street
(800) 523-5002 or (505) 982-5511, $$$$
lafondasantafe.com

The oldest hotel site in town, La Fonda features hand-painted furniture, beamed ceilings and wrought-iron light fixtures in each of its 167 rooms. In 1998, La Fonda completed La Terraza, a rooftop garden featuring 14 private luxury rooms and suites. The lobby is bustling all day long, and the bar is filled with music every night. La Fonda is truly a terrific Santa Fe experience.

La Posada de Santa Fe Resort and Spa
330 East Palace Avenue
(800) 727-5276 or (505) 986-0000, $$$$
laposadadesantafe.com
laposada.rockresorts.com/info/spa.asp

La Posada is one of Santa Fe's loveliest hotels. Built around the Staab mansion (1870s), the hotel is located on six prime acres of land only a few blocks from the Plaza. Now encompassing 159 rooms with *kiva* fireplaces and patios, it is a true oasis right in the center of town. La Posada spa, Avanyu, is noted in the chapter on shopping and spas.

HISTORIC AND OUT OF TOWN

Bishop's Lodge
Bishop's Lodge Road (10 minutes from downtown,
call for directions)
(800) 732-2240 or (505) 983-6377, $$$$
bishopslodge.com

Secluded in its own private valley in the foothills of the Sangre de Cristo Mountains, this exquisite hideaway has been ranked by *Travel & Leisure* as one of America's top 100 hotels and resorts, as well as by *Condé Nast Traveler* as one of the 500 best places to stay in the whole world. Established in 1851 as a retreat for Jean Baptiste Lamy, Bishop's Lodge has become New Mexico's vacation playground. In addition to luxurious accommodations, the resort offers lush gardens, fishing, hiking, tennis courts, horseback riding, swimming pool, fabulous spa, wellness center and nearby golf and skiing. Add to all this a fabulous restaurant and you have a vacation destination that would be hard to beat anywhere!

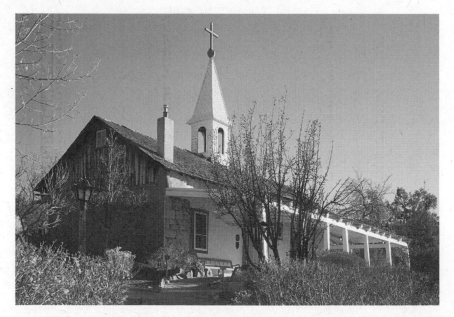

Bishop Lamy's Chapel at Bishop Lodge. Originally a retreat for Archbishop Jean Baptiste Lamy, it is now a first class hotel in the country, but minutes from Santa Fe.

Encantado, an Auberge Resort
198 State Road 592 (15 minutes from downtown,
call for directions)
(877) 262-4666, $$$$
encantadoresort.com

A new addition to the Auberge Resort group, it has 65 luxury casitas, a main lodge with the Terra Restaurant, lounge and meeting space. It also includes a 10,000-square-foot spa and pool.

Sunrise Springs Inn & Retreat
242 Los Pinos Road (about 20 minutes from downtown,
call for directions)
(800) 955-0028 or (505) 471-3600, $$$$
sunrisesprings.com

This retreat is not historical, but its uniqueness suggests its inclusion in this book. Overnight guests enjoy accommodations to enhance the spirit, including outdoor hot tubs, Japanese tea, massage/wellness services and spa, sweat lodge, raku pottery-making, wondrous gardens, ceremonial circles, pathways for exercise and meditation.

OTHER WELL-KNOWN HOTELS

Santa Fe, being famous for its hospitality as well as its history, also boasts some world-class hotels of recent origin. In spite of being relatively new, these hotels manage to create the ambience of Old Santa Fe as well as—and in some cases better than—the older places. Several of these newer hotels are world-renowned and need to be included in this book.

Eldorado Hotel
309 West San Francisco Street
(800) 286-6755 or (505) 988-4455, $$$$
eldoradohotel.com

Santa Fe's first AAA four-diamond, four-star hotel is located next to the Plaza. This upscale hotel features rooms with fireplaces and mountain views as well as two restaurants, the critically acclaimed Old House and the Eldorado Court.

Hotel Santa Fe
1501 Paseo de Peralta
(800) 825-9876 or (505) 982-1200, $$$$
hotelsantafe.com

Owned by Picuris Pueblo, Santa Fe's only Native American-owned hotel offers both comfort and culture. The hotel sits just off the Plaza and occupies three acres adorned by Native American sculpture and totems, wildflowers and privacy. Its restaurant, Amaya, features Native foods and, when weather permits, Indian dancing outdoors on the patio.

Inn and Spa at Loretto
211 Old Santa Fe Trail
(800) 727-5531 or (505) 988-5531, $$$$

hotelloretto.com

Situated next to the historic Loretto Chapel, the Inn at Loretto features interior wall murals, carved ceilings, and door frames that incorporate

Inn and Spa at Loretto. Although a modern hotel, its exterior and interior exudes the warmth of old Santa Fe.

designs, petroglyphs and weavings found in Pueblo and Spanish artistry. The hotel's fine-dining restaurant Luminaria serves breakfast, lunch and dinner. In 2002 the hotel opened SpaTerre, offering unique spa treatments as well as the usual spa amenities.

Inn of the Anasazi
113 Washington Avenue
(800) 688-8100 or (505) 988-3030, $$$$
innoftheanasazi.com

A four-diamond, four-star hotel, the Inn of the Anasazi was built in 1991 and designed as an artful blend of Southwestern culture and luxurious amenities. Handcrafted furnishings, four-poster beds and gas-lit fireplaces are framed under traditional ceilings of *vigas* and *latillas*. In the 1930s and early 1940s this site was a boarding house where some "Manhattan Project" workers stayed. After that it was home to the State Securities Company. Located steps from the Plaza, the hotel also boasts one of Santa Fe's most highly rated restaurants.

Inn of the Governors
101 West Alameda Street
(800) 234-4534 or (505) 982-4333, $$-$$$
innofthegovernors.com

Located just two blocks off the Plaza, Inn of the Governors features rooms with special touches such as Mexican folk art, kiva fireplaces, colorful painted lamps, handcrafted desks, trunks and armoires. This hotel features a complimentary full breakfast and the Del Charro Saloon, which offers light foods and desserts.

Plaza Hotel Real
125 Washington Avenue
(877) 901-ROOM or (505) 988-4900, $$$$
hhandr.com/pla_main.php

Minutes from the Plaza, Plaza Hotel Real is a picturesque boutique hotel featuring wood-burning fireplaces and handcrafted furniture and art. The hotel also is home to Jesse's Wood-Fired Pizza and Spirits and, in the summer, an outdoor *fajita* grill.

OTHER PLACES TO STAY

As mentioned at the beginning of this chapter, there are many other places to stay in Santa Fe, places that may suit your needs just fine, even though they may lack the historical sensibilities of those listed above. Santa Fe has most of the big hotel chains as well as many smaller independent motels, mainly located along Cerrillos Road. Besides the usual sources such as AAA, travel brochures, membership plans or credit-card promotions, you can find many places to stay (and restaurants, attractions and events as well) on the following websites:

Noncommercial sites

You can make reservations at almost any lodging establishment from these sites. They contain no commercial messages.

- santafe.org - official Santa Fe site for visitors, noncommercial— businesses do not pay for their listings, very complete, links to websites, includes descriptions of places
- sfdetours.com/accommodations - Santa Fe Detours reservation service, all lodgings, reservations by phone or e-mail—select your accommodation by price, etc.

Membership or group sites

You either need to be a member and use a password to enter site, or listings include only that site's own members, or managed properties:

- aaa-newmexico.com/travel - AAA reservations statewide, for AAA members nationwide
- nmhotels.com - New Mexico Lodging Association site, reservations statewide, listings are members of NMLA, commercial
- casasdesantafe.com - Casas de Santa Fe, rental of furnished homes by night or week

Commercial sites

Lodging establishments pay to be listed on these sites, and some have other commercial messages.

- www.santafe.net/accommodations - a directory of websites for hotels, motels, B&Bs, vacation rentals, etc.

- www.santafe.worldweb.com - Santa Fe Tourism World Wide Web travel guide, commercial
- www.santafescene.com - Santa Fe Scene online tourist guide, commercial, includes a wide variety of info
- santafestation.com - includes dining guide and calendars of events, commercial
- www.nmtravel.com - hotel and lodging reservations for whole state of New Mexico, emphasis on Albuquerque Balloon Fiesta, commercial
- www.santafehotels.com; www.santafecentralres.com - Santa Fe hotels, certain lodgings only, commercial, includes Web cam
- www.santafe.com - lodging, dining, events, arts and culture
- www.visitsantafe.com - listings and links for accommodations and restaurants sorted by type, also activities, the arts and maps
- www.thesantafesite.com - very informative site with info on wide variety of subjects, sponsors in web links
- www.santafeinformation.com - similar to other general information sites above, but includes a webcam
- www.sfaol.com - Santa Fe Always On Line, similar to above sites, more of a magazine format

GALLERIES, SHOPPING AND SPAS

We have observed that shopping in Santa Fe is a way of life for most visitors! And, we know that at the end of a shopping day, a person may well long for a whirlpool, a swim or a deep massage. After such pampering, one should be ready for yet another day of shopping, sightseeing and gallery hopping.

Our "shopping list" takes in an array of places we think you will enjoy. The list includes art and photography galleries, shops and museums offering Native American art and antiquities, stores that specialize in Western furniture and Western wear, and museums and bookstores where you'll find volumes on the Southwest.

Above: Nedra Matteucci Galleries. The garden is a verdant oasis filled with magnificent sculpture.

Put on your walking shoes, because most of these places can be reached on foot from your lodgings. These are just some of the many wonderful shops located all over Santa Fe. Check the Yellow Pages of the telephone book for a full list.

Before heading out to the galleries, you might like to visit them on line. You can do so with the help of this book and by using the following site:

- collectorsguide.com - *Collectors Guide*, arts magazine covering Albuquerque, Santa Fe and Taos, features extensive links to gallery sites

GALLERIES
Two of Santa Fe's Oldest and Finest Collections of Art

Gerald Peters Gallery
1011 Paseo de Peralta
(505) 954-5700
gpgallery.com

For over 30 years, the Gerald Peters Gallery has been showing museum-quality art and sculpture. Located in a new building designed in the adobe Pueblo Revival style, the gallery takes you on a perfectly splendid stylistic tour in its 8,500 feet of exhibition space. In the centerpiece gallery are works by Taos Society of Artists and the Santa Fe Colony. Other galleries display 20th-century European and American modernists, wildlife art and photography. It's easy to spend time here; take a moment to peruse the in-depth art bookstore as well. The outdoor sculpture garden features a lovely lawn, fine stonework, a beautiful waterfall and an ever-changing array of sculpture.

Nedra Matteucci Galleries
1075 Paseo de Peralta
(505) 982-4631
matteucci.com

In the 1900s, this gallery was a farm situated along a dusty road. It was expanded over a period of time to become an art gallery owned by

Gerald Peters Gallery. At first glance, you might think this is another museum in town. From its scope and breadth it could well be, except that everything is for sale.

the painter Nicolas Wolashuk. In 1972, the property was sold to Rex Arrowsmith and Forrest Fenn and was turned into the beautiful gallery it is today. Arrowsmith and Fenn specialized in the Taos Society of Artists; Western collectibles were and are featured today.

In 1988 the gallery was sold to Nedra Matteucci, who introduced contemporary painters into the mix. She expanded the beautiful (some say, the most beautiful) outdoor sculpture garden. Sculptures by Doug Hyde, Don Ostermiller and Glenna Goodacre may be enjoyed in this pastoral setting featuring a large, romantic pond, verdant trees and a softly running waterfall.

Venerable Art Galleries of Canyon Road

Altermann Galleries & Auctioneers
225 Canyon Road
(505) 983-1590
altermann.com

Canfield Gallery
414 Canyon Road
(505) 988-4199
canfieldgallery.com

The Meyer-Munson Gallery
225 Canyon Road
(505) 983-1657
munsongallery.com

Robert Nichols Gallery
419 Canyon Road
(505) 982-2145
robertnicholsgallery.com
Contemporary pottery, Native American and wood fired

Pachamama
223 Canyon Road
(505) 983-4020
Spanish Colonial antiques and folk art

Ventana Fine Art
400 Canyon Road
(505) 983-8815
ventanafineart.com

Zaplin-Lampert Gallery
651 Canyon Road
(505) 982-6100
zaplinlampert.com

Other Fine Santa Fe Galleries

Charles Azbell Gallery
203 Canyon Road
(505) 988-1875

Gebert Contemporary
558 Canyon Road
(505) 992-0711

Gebert Contemporary—Railyard
544 South Guadalupe Street
(505) 983-3838

Chiaroscuro Gallery
439 Camino Del Monte Sol
702-1/2 and 708 Canyon Road
(505) 992-0711
gebertcontemporary.com

Allan Houser Gallery
125 Lincoln Avenue
(505) 982-4705
allanhouser.com
*Representing the Estate of Allan Houser, one of the premier
Indian sculptors of the 20th century*

Charlotte Jackson Fine Art
554 South Guadalupe (in the Railyard Art District)
(505) 989-8688
charlottejackson.com
Contemporary art

Lewallen Contemporary
129 West Palace Avenue
(505) 988-8997

Lewallen Galleries at the Railyard
1613 Paseo de Peralta
(505) 988-3427
lewallencontemporary.com

Davis Mather Folk Art Gallery
141 Lincoln Avenue
(505) 983-1660
New Mexican and Mexican Folk Art

Niman Fine Art
125 Lincoln Avenue
(505) 988-5091
namingha.com
Representing Dan Namingha and the Namingha family

Owings Dewey Fine Art
120 East Marcy Street
(505) 986-9088
owingsdewey.com

Peyton-Wright
237 East Palace Avenue
(505) 999-9888
peytonwright.com

Riva Yares Gallery
123 Grant Avenue
(505) 984-0330
rivayaresgallery.com

Photography Galleries

Monroe Gallery of Photography. A first class gallery in Santa Fe, featuring photographers of the 20th Century.

Monroe Gallery of Photography
112 Don Gaspar Avenue
(505) 992-0800
monroegallery.com

Photogenesis
100 East San Francisco Street, in La Fonda
(505) 989-9540
photogenesisgallery.com

Scheinbaum and Russek Ltd.
Call for appointment, (505) 988-5116
photographydealers.com

Andrew Smith Gallery
122 Grant Avenue
(505) 986-3896
andrewsmithgallery.com

*Andrew Smith Gallery. Vintage photography showing luminaries
like Ansel Adams and Laura Gilpin.*

Verve Fine Arts. This is the place to visit for award winning contemporary photography.

Verve Fine Arts
219 East Marcy Street
(505) 424-6389
santafephotogallery.com/

Out of Town, but Worth a Visit

Shidoni
Foundry, Sculpture
Gallery and Gardens
Bishop's Lodge Road, close
to the village of Tesuque
(505) 988-8001
shidoni.com

Shidoni Sculpture Garden. A most unique garden, part of the Shidoni Foundry.

SHOPPING
Guadalupe District

The Railyard Park and Plaza
(at the train depot on Guadalupe Street)
railyardcc.org

Santa Fe has a new tourist venue. The Railyard Park and Plaza as discussed in Divas and Diversion is a mix of a farmers' market, park space, museums, boutique, restaurants and first-class art galleries.

On February 9, 1880, an Atchison, Topeka railroad train chugged into Santa Fe, putting an end to the necessity for the Santa Fe Trail (1821-1880) that delivered goods from Missouri.

The train was on a spur line (the "Chili Line") instead of the main line because of Santa Fe's inaccessibility created by mountain ranges.

In 1994 the City of Santa Fe bought the historic fifty-acre railyard district. Once a thriving active part of the community, it had been reduced over the years to one restaurant, some shops and the old railroad station.

Completely revitalized and opened in September 2008, the new "Railyard Park and Plaza" complex boasts the Market Station that has 407

Santa Fe Railroad Station. The original station is now part of the Railyard and Park project, soon to be a visitor's center.

underground parking spaces (a "must" in Santa Fe), and stores and restaurants anchored by REI, a leading outdoor gear retailer.

The old Sears Warehouse was replaced by the Railyard Galleries. In addition, look for the permanent home of the Santa Fe Farmers' Market (open on designated days, year round); Warehouse 21, a teen center for music and art; El Museo Cultural de Santa Fe, a mixed use gallery and theater; and SITE Santa Fe, a nonprofit contemporary art museum with a national reputation.

Plan on spending a good deal of time there. Take a stroll through the park setting. Note the bicycle and walking paths and children's playground and gardens. Tomasita's, The Flying Star and Second Street Brewery are there for your dining.

Walk or drive over to the Railyard, just blocks from the Plaza, for a new and different kind of Santa Fe experience.

Sanbusco Market Center
500 Montezuma Avenue
(505) 989-9390
sanbusco.com

If walls could talk, this building would recount some fascinating stories! Built in 1882, it was for many years part of Santa Fe's warehouse area. A 1980s renovation elevated the esthetics of the place and consequently its spirit: there's a lot going on here! You'll find excellent restaurants and wildly diverse shopping—divine temptations of all kinds.

The Plaza

From ancient Native artifacts to the quirkiest tourist kitsch, from designer boutiques to eclectic imports, from books to toys to postcards to— you name it! You'll find it all on or near the Plaza. In fact, perhaps the best place in town to buy Indian arts and crafts is right there, outdoors under the *portal* of the Palace of the Governors.

Buying Native Arts & Jewelry

The Santa Fe area presents many opportunities to purchase the best in Indian arts and crafts. Check the Pueblo events schedule. Arts-and-crafts fairs are held in conjunction with many of these events, so you can visit a pueblo, enjoy some colorful Native dancing and do some shopping all in one trip. Larger fairs, such as Indian Market and the Eight Northern Indian Pueblos Council Artists and Craftsmen Show, present excellent opportunities to see and purchase some of the finest Indian art available. To learn more about what to look for and about individual artists, see these websites:

- newmexicoindianart.org/buyingart.html
- ciaccouncil.org

The *Portal* at the Palace of the Governors
newmexicoindianart.org

As we stated, the *portal* at the Palace of the Governors is perhaps the very best place in town to buy Indian jewelry. The New Mexico Native American artists are licensed by the museum. You can meet the artists and buy direct, and you can "discuss" the price. The rules vendors must follow emphasize authenticity (a maker's mark is required on all goods), traditional materials, and handmade work produced as generations of Native artisans have created it. You can count on the quality, and the artists will be happy to tell you how each piece was created.

Shops for Native Arts & Jewelry

Adobe Gallery
221 Canyon Road
(505) 955-0550
adobegallery.com

Andrea Fisher Fine Pottery
100 West San Francisco Street
(505) 986-1234
andreafisherpottery.com

Keshi The Zuni Connection (fetishes)
227 Don Gaspar Avenue
(505) 989-8728
keshi.com

The Andrea Fisher Fine Pottery Gallery carries some of the finest examples of Pueblo pottery.

Ortega's on the Plaza
101 West San Francisco Street
(505) 988-1866

Packard's
61 Old Santa Fe Trail
(505) 983-9241
carries jewelry, pottery and Indian blankets

The Rainbow Man
107 East Palace Avenue
(505) 982-8706
therainbowman.com
carries American Indian antiquities as well

The Rancho de Chimayó Collection
Sena Plaza Galleries, 127 East Palace Avenue
(505) 988-4526
ranchochimayo.com

The Rainbow Man carries an amazing array of Indian antiquities.
Ask them what history transpired there.

Sources for American Indian Antiquities

Steve Elmore Indian Art
839 Paseo de Peralta
(505) 996-9677
elmoreindianart.com

Kania-Ferrin Gallery
(505) 982-8767
kaniaferringallery.com

Nedra Matteucci Galleries
1075 Paseo de Peralta
(505) 982-4631
matteucci.com

Morning Star Gallery
513 Canyon Road
(505) 982-8187
morningstargallery.com

Relics of the Old West
402 Old Santa Fe Trail
(505) 989-7663

Sherwood's Spirit of America
1005 Paseo de Peralta
(505) 988-1776
sherwoodsspirit.com

Shiprock Trading Company
53 Old Santa Fe Trail
(505) 982-8478
shiprocktrading.com

Michael Smith Gallery
526 Canyon Road
(505) 995-1013
michaelsmithgallery.com

Mark Sublette Medicine Man Gallery
200 Canyon Road
(505) 820-7451
medicinemangallery.com

Museum Shops

The following site is the gateway to all four shops run by the Museum
of New Mexico:
• shopmuseum.com
Following are the names and addresses of all the museum shops:

Museum of Indian Arts & Culture Shop
710 Camino Lejo
(505) 982-5057
miaclab.org/visit/indexs.html

Palace of the Governors Shop
105 West Palace Avenue
(505) 982-3016

New Mexico History Museum Shop
116 Lincoln Avenue
(505) 982-3016

New Mexico Museum of Art Shop
107 West Palace Avenue
(505) 476-5072

Museum of International Folk Art Shop
706 Camino Lejo
(505) 476-1200
Case Trading Post

Wheelwright Museum of the American Indian
704 Camino Lejo
(505) 982-4636
casetradingpost.com

Cowboy Boots and Other Stuff

Back at the Ranch Cowboy Boots
209 East Marcy Street
(888) 96BOOTS or (505) 989-8110
backattheranch.com

Boot Barn
Santa Fe Place
(505) 471-8775

Desert Son of Santa Fe
725 Canyon Road
(505) 982-9499

Double Take at the Ranch
319 South Guadalupe Street
(505) 820-7775

Lucchese
57 Old Santa Fe Trail
(800) 871-1883 or (505) 820-1883
lucchese.com

Montecristi Custom Hat Works
322 McKenzie Street
(505) 983-9598
montecristihats.com

O'Farrell Hats
111 East San Francisco Street
ofarrellhatco.com

Canyon Road Hats by Kevin
725 Canyon Road
(505) 989-9666

James Reid Ltd.
114 East Palace Avenue
(505) 988-1147
jrltd.com
jewelry, belts and buckles

Relics of the Old West
402 Old Santa Fe Trail
(505) 989-7663

Rio Bravo Trading Co.
411 South Guadalupe Street
(505) 982-0230

Santa Fe Boot Co.
60 E. San Francisco Street, Suite 212
(505) 989-1168
santafebootco.com

Tom Taylor
La Fonda
(505) 984-2232
tomtaylorbuckles.com
cowboy belts

Books and Maps

All the museums in town have large collections of books in their respective fields for sale in their shops. If you can't find what you want, try one of the bookshops.

The Ark Spiritual Bookstore
133 Romero Street
(505) 988-3709
arkbooks.com

Borders Books & Music
3513 Zafarano Drive
(505) 474-9450
bordersstores.com

Collected Works Bookstore
202 Galisteo Street
(505) 988-4226
collectedworksbookstore.com

Garcia Street Books
376 Garcia Street
(505) 986-0151
garciastreetbooks.com/

On-line Bookstore
booksupermart.com

Photo-Eye Books and Prints
376 Garcia Street
(505) 988-5152
photoeye.com

Travel Bug
839 Paseo de Peralta
(505) 992-0418
mapsofnewmexico.com
international guides, maps, GPS units

Distinctive Jewelry, Clothing and Accessories
(with emphasis on Southwestern and the eclectic)

La Bodega
667 Canyon Road
(505) 982-8043

Bodhi Bazaar
Sanbusco Market Center, 500 Montezuma Avenue
(505) 982-3880

Dust in The Wind
134 West Water Street
(505) 986-1155

Faircloth & Company
110 West San Francisco Street
(505) 984-1419

Gusterman Silversmiths
26 East Palace Avenue
(505) 982-8972

Lewallen & Lewallen
105 East Palace Avenue
(505) 983-2657
lewallenjewelry.com

Karen Melfi Collection
225 Canyon Road
(505) 982-3032
karenmelfi.com

Mimosa
52 Lincoln Avenue
(505) 982-5492

Nathalie
503 Canyon Road
(505) 982-1021
nathaliesantafe.com
cowboy stuff and furnishings, especially for the ladies

Origins
135 West San Francisco Street
(505) 988-2323
originssantafe.com

Purple Sage
110 Don Gaspar Avenue
(505) 984-0600
purplesagesantafe.com

James Reid Ltd.
114 East Palace Avenue
(505) 988-1147
jrltd.com

Barbara Rosen Antique Jewelry
213 West San Francisco Street
(505) 992-3000
barbararosen.com

Santa Fe Dry Goods
55 Old Santa Fe Trail
(505) 983-8142

Spirit of the Earth
108 Don Gaspar Avenue
(505) 988-9558
spiritoftheearth.com

Tresa Vorenberg
656 Canyon Road
(505) 988-7215
tvgoldsmiths.com

Distinctive Shoe Shops

Goler Fine Imported Shoes
125 East Palace Avenue
(505) 982-0924
golershoes.com

On Your Feet
Sanbusco Market Center
530 Montezuma Avenue
(505) 983-3900

Street Feet
La Fonda Hotel
(505) 984-2828
streetfeetsantafe.com

Home Furnishings, Architectural Elements and Miscellaneous

American Country Collection
620 Cerrillos Road
(505) 984-0955
53 Old Santa Fe Trail
(505) 982-1296
accsantafe.com
antiques, home furnishings

Antique Warehouse
530 South Guadalupe Street, Suite B
(505) 984-1159
antiquewarehouse-santafe.com
Spanish colonial antiques, old doors, windows, gates

Santa Fe Arius Art Tile
1800 Second Avenue
(505) 988-8966

La Fonda
(505) 988-1125
ariustile.com
fine hand-crafted art tile and murals

Artesanos Imports
1414 Maclovia Street
(505) 471-8020
artesanos.com
tiles, ceramic sinks, iron work for the home

Carpinteros (formerly Taos Furniture)
217 Galisteo Street
(505) 988-1229
taosfurniture.com
carpinteros.com
customized Southwestern furniture

Doodlet's Shop
120 Don Gaspar Avenue
(505) 983-3771

An eclectic blend of genuine antiques and reproductions of old toys, books, jewelry, folk art, signs, old-fashioned candies and greeting cards. Perfect for youngsters and oldsters alike.

El Paso Imports
419 Sandoval Street
(505) 982-5698
elpasoimportco.com

Far Eastern and Mexican Furniture—much of it crafted from old wooden pieces

Jackalope
2820 Cerrillos Road
(505) 471-8539
jackalope.com

"Everything under the sun," mainly Mexican imports and pottery

La Puerta
4523 State Highway 14
(505) 984-8164
lapuertaoriginals.com

old doors and furniture designed from old wooden pieces from all over the globe

Santa Fe Country Furniture
1708 Cerrillos Road
(505) 984-1478
Southwest furniture

*Seret & Sons is filled with pillows, Tibetan furniture, rugs,
doors and more.*

Spanish Pueblo Doors
1091 Sller Road
(505) 473-0464
spdoors.com
classic Southwest door reproductions

Susan's Christmas Shop
115 East Palace Avenue
(505) 983-2127
susanschristmasshop.com
original and handmade Christmas decorations

Outdoor Clothing and Equipment
*(should you need to buy gear for
that special hike)*

REI
Market Station at the Railyard
500 Market Street
(505) 982-3557
rei.com

Sangre de Cristo Mountain Works
328 South Guadalupe
(505) 984-8221
sdcmountainworks.com

SPAS

Slip into a spa after a day of doing Santa Fe!

Absolute Nirvana
Spa, Tea Room and Gardens
106 Faithway Street
(505) 983-7942
absolutenirvana.com

Nestled in a Victorian house, just off Palace Avenue is a most unusual spa. Combining Indonesian Spa treatments, rose petal bath and Thai hot stone massage with a quaint tearoom setting amid beautiful gardens, it is different in every way.

Avanyu Spa at La Posada de Santa Fe
330 East Palace
(505) 986-0000 or (505) 954-9630
laposada.rockresorts.com/info/spa.asp

This new spa is located on La Posada Resort grounds, just a few blocks from the Plaza. Its state-of-the-art massage center offers skin-care treatments and specialty bodywork, a fitness center, an outdoor heated pool and a whirlpool.

Genoveva Chávez Community Center
3321 Rodeo Road
(505) 955-4001 or (505) 955-4002,
call for information and directions
gccommunitycenter.com

If you're in the mood for a good old-fashioned workout, then the new Chávez Center is for you. It's workout heaven here with an Olympic-size pool, a full gym, a running track and an NHL regulation-size hockey and figure-skating rink. You can even rent ice skates! If you need a massage, that can be arranged with an advance call. Owned by the city, the Chávez center offers very reasonable rates for daily admission. Truly a Santa Fe jewel.

Ojo Caliente Mineral Springs
North on U.S. 285
50 Los Baños Drive, Ojo Caliente
(800) 222-9162 or (505) 583-2233
ojocalientespa.com

New Mexicans have enjoyed this spa for decades. One of the oldest health resorts in North America, it was considered a sacred spot by the Pueblo Indians who inhabited the area. These are the only natural hot springs in the world containing a specific mixture of iron, lithia, soda, arsenic and sodium. Besides a good soak, you may avail yourself of therapeutic massage and facial treatments, yoga instruction and guided meditations, art workshops, a restaurant, gift shop, hiking trails and hotel and cottage lodging.

• Open seven days a week, call for hours.

ShàNah Spa at Bishop's Lodge
Bishop's Lodge Road (10 minutes from downtown, call for directions)
(505) 983-6377 or (800) 732-2240
bishopslodge.com
shanahspa.com/shanah
bishopslodge.com/Shanah

The ShàNah Spa at The Bishop's Lodge is located in the lush foothills just north of Santa Fe, which is steeped deep within the Native American traditions and home of some of the oldest Spanish settlements in America. With these strong traditions, ShàNah makes use of natural healing remedies, herbs, sweat baths and teas. They aim to customize the treatment to each individual, invoking the body's natural healing response. From Native Stone Massage to the Tesuque Clay Wrap, Abiyanga to Desert Fusion, the treatments go beyond your highest expectations.

SpaTerre
At Inn and Spa at Loretto
24 Old Santa Fe Trail
(505) 984-7997
innatloretto.com/loretto_spaterre.aspx

This centrally located spa offers a refuge that promotes health and well-being for mind, body and soul. Treatments come from exotic Bali, Java, and Thailand as well as Swedish and Nature Desert massages. It offers a fitness center as well as Yoga.

Sunrise Springs Inn & Retreat
242 Los Pinos Road, La Cienega
(505) 471-3600, call for information and rates
sunrisesprings.com/spa_samadhi

This laid-back spot is only 12 miles from Santa Fe, but you'd swear you'd traveled more like 12,000 miles! The feeling is Far Eastern, and the emphasis is on massage, yoga and ancient wellness treatments. The accommodations are lovely, and the views are beautiful.

Tamaya Mist Spa
Hyatt Regency Tamaya Resort & Spa
1300 Tuyuna Trail, Santa Ana Pueblo
(800) 633-7313 or (505) 867-1234
tamaya.hyatt.com/hyatt/hotels

The Pueblo-style, luxurious 16,000-square-foot spa features specialty treatments, massage, skin treatments and more. It also offers a well-equipped fitness center and a beautiful yoga/aerobic wellness theater. Separate men's and women's meditation, sauna/steam and changing areas add to the relaxed enjoyment of this world-class spa. In addition to luxury spa treatments, it offers many specialty classes and programs, including yoga instruction, specialized fitness classes, one-on-one personal training, tai chi and meditation events.

Ten Thousand Waves
3451 Hyde Park Road
(505) 982-9304, call for directions and hours
tenthousandwaves.com

We first found this particularly wonderful spa in the mid-1980s. I well remember our private room—open to the beauty of the Sangre de Cristo Mountains—and the satisfying hot tub and superb Swedish massage that followed.

Ten Thousand Waves has since evolved into a state-of-the-art Japanese health spa with all the amenities—therapeutic massages as well as specialized types including Masters, Thai, Japanese Hot Stone and Four Hands (two therapists working in union). Healthy snacks and drinks can be purchased along with creams and lotions, candles and cotton kimonos. Oh my!

This is primarily a day spa, but with luck, you may be able to reserve one of their luxurious guest suites at the Houses of the Moon—the closest accommodations to the Santa Fe Ski Area.

Encantado, an Auberge Resort
198 State Road 592 (15 minutes from downtown, call for directions)
(877) 262-4666
encantadoresort.com

This new hotel is part of Auberge Resort group. The Spa offers classic massages, as well as those regionally inspired, Ayurvedic and traditional Eastern medicine. Special attention to men and couples.

Vista Clara Ranch Resort and Spa
Route 41, Galisteo
(888) 663-9772 or (505) 466-4772
Call for information, rates and directions
vistaclara.com

About one-half hour out of Santa Fe, just outside the tiny artsy village of Galisteo you'll find the Vista Clara Ranch. Vista Clara offers upscale lodging and gourmet cuisine complementing its spa treatments and therapies, an ozone pool, jacuzzi, Swiss showers, art classes and a sweat lodge . . . the works. And don't forget hiking, horseback riding and a gym—if you've got the strength. You can even arrange for a limo to pick you up and take you home. Wow!

SIDE TRIPS TO THE COUNTRY

One of the best parts of visiting Santa Fe is the variety of "must do" day trips out into the surrounding countryside. You'll come away with an enhanced sense of local history and some treasured memories of the beauty of the land. We're aware that your visit here may be a short one, and thus have only listed those trips that are reasonably close to Santa Fe. Onward!

- newmexico.org
- newmexico.org/outdoors

ABIQUIÚ

Most of us have become aware of the beauty of the hills and canyons of Abiquiú through the landscape paintings of Georgia O'Keeffe. The Abiquiú area is most assuredly a fine day's trip.

From Santa Fe, take U.S. 285 north to Española. At Española pick up U.S. 84 North and follow it toward Abiquiú. After reaching Abiquiú, you will enter a 15-miles stretch that encompasses Ghost Ranch and the world of Georgia O'Keeffe.

- okeeffemuseum.org/background

O'Keeffe was artistically inspired by Abiquiú and in 1949 moved there permanently. Long before she arrived, legends of witches or *brujos* were widely circulated. In Lesley Poling-Kempes' wonderful history book, *Valley of Shining Stone: The Story of Abiquiú*, she notes:

In a region already rich in superstition—the local lore of the Piedra Lumbre included tales of a flying cow who heralded not just insanity but also imminent death, and an oft repeated legend of a giant, child-eating snake that emerged from the earth near the red cliffs at sundown—the Archuleta brothers and their homestead beneath the cliffs of Shining Stone would earn legendary status . . . they chose this hidden canyon with its singular southern entrance and sheer rock walls because of its natural characteristic as a holding and hiding pen for cattle. According to local legend the Archuleta brothers herded stolen cattle through the mountains by day and the valleys by night to their secluded, natural rock canal in Yeso Canyon . . . out of towners who stopped for the night for what they thought was friendly and welcomed lodging . . . never emerged in the morning and their horses and personal effects were suddenly counted among the Archuletas' tack and livestock. The corpses of the victims were believed to be at the bottom of the homestead well. The Rito del Yeso homestead was soon given a new name: Rancho de los Brujos, or Witch Ranch, or Ghost Ranch. (Poling-Kempes, p. 129)

That piece of land is still Ghost Ranch. It is now owned by the Presbyterian Church, which operates it as a conference center. Georgia O'Keeffe had a home at Ghost Ranch named Rancho de los Burros. Ghost Ranch mainly hosts conferences, but individual rooms may be available.
- For inquires call (505) 685-4333 or access the Ghost Ranch website: ghostranch.org

Georgia O'Keeffe had another, more famous home in Abiquiú itself. She lived there from 1949 to 1984. It is now run by the O'Keeffe Foundation, which conducts limited tours of the 7,000-square-foot adobe. The simplicity of the house and its rooms reflect the aesthetic soul of the artist. Tours are by reservation only and must be scheduled well in advance. They are held on Tuesdays, Thursdays and Fridays from April through November, generally for up to 12 people. A fee donation of $22 is requested and is tax deductible.
- For further information contact: Georgia O'Keeffe Foundation, P.O. Box 40, Abiquiú, NM 87510, (505) 685-4539; cr.nps.gov/nr/feature/wom/1999/o'keeffe.htm

After 1984 O'Keeffe moved to Santa Fe to be closer to medical facilities.

Her estate, called "Sol y Sombre" (Sun and Shade), was occupied until her death in 1986 at age 98.

Also of interest in Abiquiú is the Monastery of Christ in the Desert, run by the Subiaco Monastic Community headquartered in Rome, Italy. It is a simple retreat with a lovely church and a refectory adorned with magnificent religious frescoes. The original church architect is George Nakashima, a world-renowned artist.

- christdesert.org

In Abiquiú, the Abiquiú Inn has been a welcome respite from touring since 1985, offering lodging, an RV park and a pleasant restaurant.

- Call (800)-477-5621 for information or visit abiquiuinn.com

BANDELIER NATIONAL MONUMENT

- Near Los Alamos
- (505) 672-3861

Bandelier is 46 miles (74.1 km) west of Santa Fe. Take U.S. 285 north from Santa Fe to Pojoaque, then drive west on N.M. 502 to N.M. 4 (12 miles southwest of Los Alamos).

The volcano that erupted on this land 2.4 million years ago formed one of the largest *calderas*, or depressions, in the world; the volcanic rim forms the Jemez Mountains. On these canyon-slashed slopes at the bottom of the Pajarito Plateau you will see the ruins of cliff houses called *cavates*. These are caves carved out of volcanic ash by the Pueblo Indians using basalt and obsidian tools. There are 1100 *cavates* and only one natural cave in the park. Bandelier is a 32,000-acre monument to the Anasazi who once lived there, as well as to Adolph Bandelier, a Swiss-American ethnologist who studied Southwest pueblo ruins in the late 19th century. Within Bandelier, 70 miles of trails provide access to ancient pueblos, cliff dwellings and ceremonial caves and offer as well opportunities for backpacking, bird watching, camping and picnicking. Bandelier is not to be missed!

Best Bet—Tsankawi is an unexcavated Pueblo Indian ruin on N.M. 502. This lesser known treasure is hard to find; it is just before a traffic light on the way to White Rock. Pull in off the road (but make sure you have a day pass from Bandelier, which you will display on your

Bandelier National Monument has over 1,000 caves carved out of volcanic ash by Pueblo Indians.

car dashboard). It is worth the effort. You'll follow the same ancient pathways made from volcanic ash that the Indians used and wore down. You'll explore the caves and see walls blackened from fires. Children will especially love this site. It will make them feel that they were the first to discover it.

• nps.gov/band

KASHA-KATUWE TENT ROCKS NATIONAL MONUMENT

• (800) 252-0191

To get there, take I-25 south to the Cochiti exit (264). At the end of the exit ramp, go right on N.M. 16 for 8 miles. At the "T" intersection, turn right onto N.M. 22. Go 1.7 miles and then turn right on Tribal Road 92/Forest Service Road 266. Pass through a gate and continue for 5 miles to the parking area on the right. You'll see a sign saying "Welcome to Tent Rocks." The fee is $5 per vehicle.

Kasha-Katuwe Tent Rocks National Monument has tent-like shapes of volcanic ash sculpted by the wind that would make Picasso envious.

Do you remember making those wonderful sandcastles at the beach? No matter how you tried to preserve them, the tide came in and wiped them out. Fret no more. Tent Rocks is a place where castles don't disappear. It's a place where, 6.8 million years ago, volcanic rock debris formations were sculpted into tent-like cones. Covering almost 12,000 acres, Tent Rocks is a dry place and good for hiking—to be avoided in the summer months, however, when it heats up. Try the 1.1-mile Cave Loop Hike or Canyon Trail, a 1.3-mile jaunt with a modest elevation gain. Kids will love it and so will you.

- en.wikipedia.org/wiki/Kasha-Katuwe_Tent_Rocks_National_Monument
- nm.blm.gov/recreation/albuquerque/kasha_katuwe.htm

THE TURQUOISE TRAIL

Take I-25 south to the Madrid exit (278A), moving onto N.M. 14 going south. Drive for about 20 minutes (15 miles).

As a counterbalance to "'Santa Fe adobe," why not experience a short journey out of the city to two towns that reveal another side of New Mexico? Cerrillos and Madrid (accent the Ma to pronounce it as New Mexicans do) will transport you into yet another realm of New Mexican history and architecture.

- turquoisetrail.org

Cerrillos

Cerrillos is an old mining town where people settled and dug for gold, silver, zinc and the best quality turquoise in the surrounding hills. Its quiet demeanor today hardly reveals its rowdy 1880s roots when it was filled with hotels and bars. A street or two are still reminiscent of that frontier town, but now the main attractions are a turquoise museum, a petting zoo, a trading post and a church, the Iglesia San Jose, built in 1922. A now faded sign painted on the side of a brick building—"Clear Light Opera House"—conjures up the Cerrillos of days gone by.

- turquoisetrail.org/cerrillos.htm
- cerrilloshills.org

Allan Houser Compound
(505) 471-1528

After leaving Cerrillos, continue south on N.M. 14, turning left onto N.M. 42 towards Galisteo, and in 1.5 miles you will come upon the Allan Houser Compound. To arrange a visit, call two days in advance. Tours are Monday through Saturday and cost $15 per person. Allow two hours at this remarkable place.

Allan Houser (Allan C. Haozous) was a renowned Chiricahua Apache sculptor (1914-1994). His works are to be found in numerous museums including the National Museum of American Art in Washington, D.C., The Denver Art Museum and the Heard Museum in Phoenix, Arizona. His statue, *Sacred Rain Arrow*, done in 1988, was on display during the 2002 Winter Olympics in Salt Lake City, Utah. The compound and gardens that house much of Houser's work are absolutely worth the trip.

- allanhouser.com

Madrid

This small, colorful place was originally a coal-mining town that began to boom in the 1860s. The mines uniquely produced both hard and soft coal and Madrid thrived into the World War II years when coal was much needed. By 1959, other fuels had replaced the "indispensable" coal, and the town was left with 12 people. The Old Coal Mine Museum is a worthwhile visit.

- turquoisetrail.org/oldcoalmine

In the 1970s, Madrid was reinvented by artists and craftspeople looking for an inexpensive lifestyle. Today, it boasts an artist colony of about 350 people. Reconverted miners' bungalows and once-vacant stores house the many galleries that sell art, weavings, ceramics and other crafts. Inside one gallery and bookstore, an original 1930s soda fountain is still in use. During the holidays, Madrid presents annual Christmas light displays on houses and stores, a lovely sight if you happen to be in Santa Fe for the holidays.

- mad-rid.com
- turquoisetrail.org/madrid.htm

Madrid is filled with offbeat art galleries and craft shops.

PECOS

If you are interested in seeing some magnificent scenery or in excellent fishing and hiking, take the short drive out to Pecos. Go out I-25 north to the Glorieta/Pecos exit, turn left at the top of the ramp, at the "T" intersection stop sign turn right towards Pecos (6 miles). When you get to town, you can go left and up into the mountains or right and head out to the Pecos National Monument. Or you may wish to spend some time in this old Northern New Mexico village itself!

- pecosnewmexico.com

Pecos National Historical Park

One of the most spectacular ruins to be seen anywhere in the nation, Pecos National Historical Park preserves 12,000 years of history, including the ancient Pueblo of Pecos. One of the most spectacular ruins to be seen anywhere in the nation, Pecos National Historical Park preserves 1,000 years of human history including the ancient Pueblo of Pecos and the Spanish Mission complex dating to the early 1600s. Be sure to bring your camera!

- nps.gov/peco

Pecos National Historical Park deserves a visit if you want to recapture the scope and breath of an ancient pueblo.

Glorieta National Battlefield

On the way to Pecos, you will pass though the Glorieta National Battlefield, where a major battle of the Civil War (the Battle of Glorieta Pass, known as the "Gettysburg of the Southwest") was fought. The Colorado Union troops known as "Pike's Peakers" defeated the Confederates and thereby stopped further Confederate incursions into the Southwest, preventing them from journeying on to Colorado and mining its precious gold, which would have helped finance their war effort.

- en.wikipedia.org/wiki/Battle_of_Glorieta_Pass
- americancivilwar.com/statepic/nm/nm002.html

WINERIES

New Mexico's sun-soaked soil, cool high-desert nights and ideal soil feed Cabernet Sauvignon, Chardonnay, Johannisburg Riesling, Merlot, Pinot Noir, Sauvignon Blanc, Zinfandel and other classic grapes and fruits to produce award-winning wines. Why not add dropping by a local winery to your excursion in the country? You can use this Web site to learn all about the wineries and which one may be right on your way!

- nmwine.com

THE GREAT OUT OF DOORS

The Santa Fe area is a wonderland for the outdoors enthusiast. Whatever your pleasure, from fishing to snowboarding, you can find it here.

- santafe.com/outdoors

Golf

This book was written for the short-time visitor, so I was apprehensive about putting in information on golfing in Santa Fe. But my golfing friends informed me that a golfing aficionado will always try to get in 18 holes in any city that he or she might visit, regardless of what else that city has to offer. So with that, here are some selections for nearby golf:

- golfnewmexico.com
- nmgolf.net

Black Mesa Golf Club
115 State Road 399, La Mesilla
(just outside Española)
(505) 747-8946
blackmesagolfclub.com

Owned by Santa Clara Pueblo, Northern New Mexico's newest 18-hole championship course is located about 30 miles from Santa Fe. Take U.S. 84/285 north, go west on N.M. 399 at the Dream Catcher Cinema, then turn south after less than a mile. You will find a gravel driveway and a gate that says Black Mesa. For refreshments, you can enjoy burritos and burgers at the Black Mesa Grill.

Marty Sanchez Links de Santa Fe
205 Caja del Rio
(505) 955-4400
linksdesantafe.com/

Right at the edge of town lies a beautiful public 18-hole championship course and a 9-hole par 3 course, all framed by the Sangre de Cristo, Jemez, Sandia and Ortiz mountains.

Paa-Ko Ridge Golf Club
1 Clubhouse Drive, Sandia Park
paakoinfo@paakoridge.com

Paa-Ko Ridge Golf Club is one of the most challenging and award-winning courses in the country. This 27-hole public golf course is situated on the east side of the Sandia Mountain, 45 minutes from Santa Fe. Enjoy the ride out on the Turquoise Trail.

Pueblo de Cochiti Golf Course
Cochiti Lake
(505) 464-2239
pueblodecochiti.org/golfcourse.html

This lovely golf course was designed by Robert Trent Jones, Jr., in 1981. Surrounded by the beauty of the landscape, you can play this course at a very inexpensive price. Greens fees are $35 to $50.

Santa Fe Country Club
On Airport Road, 2 miles west of Cerrillos Road
(505) 471-0601
santafecountryclub.com

The Santa Fe Country Club has a challenging 18-hole course that is now available for public play. Call for tee times and information.

Towa Golf Resort
U.S. 84/285, Pojoaque Pueblo
(12 scenic miles north of Santa Fe)
(877) 465-3489 or (505) 455-9000
towagolf.com

Towa Golf Resort offers challenging golf, amazing Southwestern vistas and first-rate service. Eighteen of the 36 holes, designed by Hale Irwin and William Phillips, are now open, as well as a first-class clubhouse and golf shop that features a full-service restaurant and bar complete with meeting facilities. Towa has become one of the top public golf courses in the Southwest. If not everyone in your party wishes to play golf, several Pueblo casinos in the area can keep them occupied!

Hiking

Remembering that this book was designed for the person on a short visit, you might feel hard-pressed to get away to the dirt, gravel and pine needles of the hiking trails of Santa Fe. But for those of you so inclined there are several hikes I would suggest. Once you get up into the Sangre de Cristos with their piñons, junipers and ponderosa pines, you will feel for certain that you're in the Rocky Mountains.

Always take water and appropriate clothing (including a hat) as the weather can change abruptly at any season of the year. Also be aware of the altitude: most of the mountain trails are considerably higher than Santa Fe's 7,000-foot elevation. As you climb, you may feel short of breath. It does take a day or two to acclimate to the altitude. Here are four of my favorite close-to-town hikes that will get you out into nature and onto the trails.

- santafe.com/outdoors/hiking.html

A hiking group making their way up a Tent Rock trail.

Atalaya Mountain

From the northeast corner of the Plaza, drive east (toward the mountains) on Palace Avenue for one mile, cross Paseo de Peralta and continue to the intersection of Palace and Alameda Street. Turn left on Alameda. A few hundred yards past Smith Park, Alameda veers right (south) and becomes Camino Cabra. Continue south on Camino Cabra past Cristo

Rey Catholic Church. About 0.7 mile past the church, you'll go by Los Miradores condo development on your left. Turn left onto Camino Cruz Blanca at the St. John's College sign. Turn right into the college and then an immediate left into the visitors' parking lot. Trailhead #174 is at the far end of the lot.

This seven-mile round trip hike begins at the parking lot right next to St. John's College. Walk at your own pace, and as you climb higher, keep turning around to enjoy the views of the Rio Grande Valley and the City of Santa Fe below you and the Jemez Mountains to the west. The trail winds through piñon and juniper, ponderosa, Douglas and white fir trees. It's about 3-1/2 miles from the parking lot to the top of Atalaya (".watchtower"), and at the top you're at 9,121 feet, with a spectacular view spread out before you. Even if you don't make it all the way to the top, you will be rewarded with magnificent views wherever you choose to stop.

Aspen Vista

From the Plaza, go north on Washington Avenue, cross Paseo de Peralta, and at the next traffic light turn right onto Artist Road. The sign here will point you to Hyde State Park and the Ski Basin. Follow this road (SH 475) 12.6 miles (uphill) from there and turn right into the parking lot with the Aspen Vista sign.

This is a wide-open trail that Santa Feans use for hiking, snowshoeing, cross-country skiing and mountain biking. It can be easy or strenuous, depending . . . the entire trail is a 12-mile round trip, but many people use it for a simple, strolling hike. It is especially beautiful in the autumn—October is best—when the aspens make their magic by turning a brilliant yellow (hence the name of the trail). Allow six hours if you're going to do the entire hike. The highest point of the trail is 12,040 feet, and the elevation gain is 2,040 feet.

Chamisa Trail

From the Plaza, go north on Washington Avenue, cross Paseo de Peralta, and at the next traffic light turn right onto Artist Road. The sign here will point you to Hyde State Park and the Ski Basin. Follow this road

(SH 475) for approximately 5.6 miles to a wide spot on the left side of the road and park there. You will find a U.S. Forest Service sign marked Trail 183—Big Tesuque 2 miles. Begin here.

This is a 4¾-mile round trip, a rather easy hike that will take you through beautiful, sweet-smelling piñon-juniper and mixed conifer vegetation belts, with a rise in elevation of 1,240 feet. Descending, you arrive at Big Tesuque Creek on the ski basin road. Be sure to bring a hat!

The Randall Davey Audubon Center
1800 Upper Canyon Road
(505) 983-4609
nm.audubon.org/audubon_center/center.html

The Center is at the end of upper Canyon Road. Head up Canyon Road and on through the residential area until you see Cristo Rey Catholic Church on your right. Turn right at the church, then turn immediately to the left and continue driving to the end of the road.

Randall Davey, one of Santa Fe's favorite painters of the early and

Randall Davey Audubon Center

mid-1900s, bought this historic old house and the 135-acre grounds in 1920. The National Audubon Society purchased the property from the Randall Davey Foundation in 1983 and now maintains the grounds as an environmental education center and wildlife refuge. The property was once a Spanish land grant; later it became a U.S. Army sawmill. Located at the mouth of the Santa Fe Canyon, the sanctuary includes miles of gorgeous hiking trails and boasts as well a small pond and wetland area, a picnic area, gardens, orchards and a lawn area. One may tour the home (reservations are necessary), peruse the small, delightful gift shop and then take to the trails to learn about the flora and fauna of Northern New Mexico.

Horseback Riding

Thoughts of the Southwest usually conjure up thoughts of cowboys, horses and wide-open spaces. Santa Fe and its environs can provide the horses should you want to get up in the saddle and ride. You can contact these places for prices and reservations:

Alta Vista Stable
54-1/2 East San Francisco Street
(505) 983-6565
sfdetours.com/horses.html

Bishop's Lodge Ranch Resort
Bishop's Lodge Road
(505) 983-6377
bishopslodge.com/resort_activities/horseback_riding.cfm
Rides from April to October

The next two can be combined with a trip down the Turquoise Trail:

Makarios Ranch
Galisteo Basin
(505) 473-1038
members.aol.com/annieokl/rides.index.html

Broken Saddle Riding Company
Off N.M. 14, Cerrillos
(505) 424-7774
brokensaddle.com

River Rafting

Santa Fe is not far from the Rio Grande and the Rio Chama. With the first rush of snowmelt in early May, the rafting and kayaking season begins and runs through the summer. Early spring brings fast water and big waves. By midsummer, the rivers calm down and the runs are easier and more playful. Rafting is a good way to take in the natural beauty of New Mexico. On the next page are some of the rafting companies to contact, should you have the inclination and the time.

Cottam's Rio Grande River Trips
207-A Paseo del Pueblo Sur, Taos
(800) 322-8267 or (505) 758-2282
Meet at Rio Grande Gorge Visitor Center
U.S. 84/285 to S.R. 68, Pilar
cottamsoutdoor.com/rafting.htm

Kokopelli Rafting
541 West Cordova Road
(800) 879-9035 or (505) 983-3734
kokopelliraft.com

Los Rios River Runners
Taos
(505) 776-8854 or (800) 544-1181
losriosriverrunners.com

New Wave Rafting Company
Route 5, Box 302A
(800) 984-1444 or (505) 984-1444
newwaverafting.com

Santa Fe Detours Rafting
54-1/2 East San Francisco Street
(888) 338-6877 or (505) 983-6565
sfdetours.com/rivers.html

Santa Fe Rafting Company & Outfitters
(800) 467-7238 or (505) 988-4914
santaferafting.com

Bird Watching

New Mexico has the fourth highest number of bird species in the country, making it a bird watcher's delight. You can hike out on your own or contact these sources for guidance.

Wingswest Birding Tours
800-583-6928
home.earthlink.net/-wingswestnm

Bill West is an enthusiastic bird guide. For example, he'll lead you on a full-day tour of Ruby Ranch and the Las Vegas National Wildlife Refuge, the ranches of San Miguel County or on shorter four-hour tours. He knows his *Sibley Guide to Birds* to perfection.

The Randall Davey Audubon Center
1800 Upper Canyon Road
(505) 983-4609
newmexicoaudubon.org

The Audubon Center offers free guided bird walks on the first and third Saturdays of each month at 9 a.m. Meet at the center's parking lot. Great for beginner or expert.

Winter Sports
Skiing and Snowboarding

Santa Fe Ski Area
(505) 983-9155 and (505) 982-4429
skisantafe.com

If you're visiting in the winter and love to ski, it's smart to be ready and bring your own skis. Or if you prefer, you can rent equipment at one of many shops in town or at the ski valley itself. Santa Fe has a jewel of a ski basin just 16 miles from the Plaza. Trails are beautifully groomed, and the snow averages 200 inches annually. Trails cater to every type of skier, and the views are magnificent.

Snowshoeing and Cross-Country Skiing

Two hiking trails mentioned previously, Chamisa Trail and Aspen Vista Trail, make ideal snowshoeing trails in the winter. Bring your own shoes or rent them at various sport shops listed in the Yellow Pages. Snowshoeing offers blessed solitude, stellar views a great aerobic workout, and, of course, the trails are free! They are also great for cross-country skiing; just remember that there isn't much flat terrain in the Santa Fe area—it's important to master the art of snowplowing for stopping on a downhill trail.

Winter Guides

Outspire Hiking and Snowshoeing
(505) 660-0394
outspire.com

Should you feel the need for a private guide, call Outspire. They will outfit you with snowshoes, poles and supply lots of hot chocolate. Outings can last from two hours to all day.

Over: Taos Pueblo, probably one of the most famous because of its multilevel dwellings.

10

TAOS

Tourists have always been lured from Santa Fe to spend at least a day in Taos. Although a much smaller town, it is similar to Santa Fe in its rich Spanish history, thriving art colony, famous Indian pueblo and, of course, its world-class ski complex.

From Santa Fe, there are two basic ways to get to Taos. The first, the Low Road along the rushing Rio Grande, and the second, the High Road, which takes you into the higher country, where you can see the small villages, visit the famous Santuario de Chimayó, and perhaps buy a beautiful weaving. The round trip can be a loop, so you can do both in a day. We recommend you start your journey by following the High Road, as it is longer and has more attractions along the way.

"You take the high road, and I'll take the low road . . ." are the words we all know from an old Scottish song—but those words can easily apply to your trip to Taos. The roads you'll travel are some of the most scenic in the United States.

- taoschamber.com
- taosguide.com
- skitaos.org

THE HIGH ROAD TO TAOS

We start by taking U.S. 84/285 north out of Santa Fe. Several miles before Española, you will come to N.M. 503. Turn right on 503, which heads north and east, and you will begin your High Road adventure! The first stop of this journey is Chimayó. Make a left turn onto N.M. 76 and follow the signs to Chimayó.

- evanderputten.org/special/newmexico/highroad.htm

Chimayó

The Santuario de Chimayó

One of the main reasons for visiting Chimayó is to see its church, the Santuario de Chimayó. A Chimayó family built this chapel around 170 years ago. It resembles Spanish mission churches, except the church is smaller, the bell towers are partly wood and a low building masks the

The Santuario de Chimayó is a must visit on the High Road to Taos tour.

front. The main roof is pitched and of corrugated metal, typical of later Northern New Mexican. The setting is very rural, with cows grazing nearby, the *acequia* (ditch) in front, the stream behind, the fruit trees in the valley and the mountains as a backdrop.

The late Edward C. Clark, a longtime resident of Santa Fe, described the Santuario de Chimayó and the town as follows:

> This chapel is no museum, no ordinary church. It is the Lourdes of the Southwest. On Good Friday, thousands of Hispanics and Indians come here, some traveling hundreds of miles. Many of them walk from Santa Fe, from Albuquerque, from even more distant spots. Nearby highways become crowded with pilgrims. Some bear heavy crosses, a few walk on their knees, most get blisters. The beaten grass, the picnic tables, the outdoor altar behind the chapel, the several nearby stores only partly reflect the crowds—it's exhilarating, not peaceful, then.
>
> Pilgrims come here to fulfill vows and to pray for cures. One focal point is a *posito*, or little well in the floor inside. Dirt scooped from that hole has long been credited with miraculous cures, perhaps even before there was a chapel. The *posito* may, in fact, perpetuate an earlier Tewa Indian belief that the site had curative powers. There is plenty of blessed dirt nearby, but on Good Friday, and in July on the feast day of Santiago (St. James), church aides are hard-pressed to keep the *posito* full.

- roadsideamerica.com/attract/NMCHIshrine.html
- archdiocesesantafe.org/AboutASF/Chimayo.html
- chimayomuseum.org

Shops and Gallery

After visiting the chapel, drive one mile north on N.M. 510. You will see a sign on the left describing Chimayó. Make a sharp left, passing in front of Ortega's Weaving Shop. Consider stopping there if you have time—their woolen weavings are a traditional Chimayó specialty.

off canada
ancha next to santory

Ortega's Weaving Shop
CR 98 at NM 76
(877) 351-4215 or (505) 351-4215
ortegasweaving.com

Plaza and Presidio

To quote the late Edward C. Clark:

> These plaza buildings, with their thick outside walls, were origi-
> nally constructed with few windows. Torreons, or defense towers,
> guarded the corners. One still stands. In case of Indian attack,
> residents could bring in the livestock, close the gates, man the
> roofs and sit tight. Water from Santa Fe's presidio came in by the
> acequia, which is still flowing. Residents could grow crops and
> store grains there. The plaza/fort could hold out until help came
> or until the Indians gave up.
>
> After the Indian raids ended, the presidio served no purpose. Peo-
> ple spread out, and a Presbyterian school and church moved in and
> made converts. Later, public schools replaced most Presbyterian
> schools, but in Chimayó the school continues to thrive. Over time,
> families divided the central plaza into ever-smaller plots. The form
> of the presidio remains, however, one of the last in the Southwest.
>
> In 1986 Robert Redford thought Chimayó the ideal spot to film
> his *Milagro Bean Field War*, an amusing tale of tradition vs. devel-
> opment in Northern New Mexico. Some residents objected, so
> Redford switched the filming to Truchas (see next page). Truchas
> made money. Chimayó kept its plaza pure. A post-Redford bum-
> per sticker reads, "Plaza del Cerro, I love you the way you are."

- chimayo.org

Centinela Traditional Arts
HCR 64, Box 4, Chimayó
(505) 351-2180

After leaving Ortega's, make a right onto Route 76 and drive for a few
miles to Centinela Traditional Arts, on the left side of the road. Irvin and
Lisa Trujillo are renowned weavers in the Rio Grande, Satillo and Vallero
style of weaving. Their tapestries have been purchased by collectors and
museums, including the Smithsonian and the Museum of International
Folk Art. Irvin was awarded the 2005 Masters Award for Lifetime Achievement by the Spanish Colonial Art Society. And in 2007 the U.S. government awarded him a National Heritage Fellowship Award. Their shop is
certainly worth a visit.

- chimayoweavers.com

Restaurante Rancho de Chimayó
County Road 98, Chimayó
(505) 351-4444 or (505) 984-2100 or
(505) 351-1211, $-$$

After returning to the highway, turn right on N.M. 520 toward the Santuario, and at 0.6 mile, turn left into Restaurante Rancho de Chimayó. The Jaramillo family made this building their home 100 years ago. Later, their descendents converted it to a restaurant. You'll find the food and atmosphere a country-style masterpiece. Enjoy the terraces out back in summer, soak up patio sunshine in spring and fall and move up to the unique double fireplace on winter evenings. Eat your fill of native dishes. Do your own looking around. It's all pleasant. It's all Chimayó.

- ranchochimayo.com/Ranchodechimayorestaurant.htm

Cordova

Now continue north on N.M. 76 through rolling hills and verdant forest. You will next approach Cordova, a small village that has gained a reputation for fine woodcarving over the years. A man named José Dolores Lopez created the unpainted "Cordova style" of carving in the 1920s. In the village, you will find many houses whose residents offer their carvings for sale. Also, the St. Anthony of Padua Chapel, filled with *retablos* (depictions of various saints painted on boards) is worth a peek.

Truchas

The next village on the High Road is Truchas (trout in Spanish). This very old, very Hispanic mountain town (founded in 1754) gained some notoriety as the location for the filming of Robert Redford's *The Milagro Beanfield War*, based on the novel by John Nichols, a New Mexican resident. The picture has become a movie classic.

Truchas has a sublimely creative soul—many artists are in residence and the town has several outstanding art galleries. The views of the Sangre de Cristo Mountains from Truchas are breathtaking.

- en.wikipedia.org/wiki/Truchas,_New_Mexico

Las Trampas

It's five miles to Las Trampas, a small town sprinkled with Northern New Mexican farmhouses and stacked woodpiles. There you'll find a wonderful mid-1700s Spanish colonial chapel, San Jose de Gracias, which holds quite a collection of religious folk art. In 1990 William de Buys and Alex Harris wrote *River of Traps*, or *Rio de las Trampas*, based on the real-life story of a village resident and his influence on the lives of the authors. If Las Trampas opens your heart, then look for the book back in Santa Fe.

- en.wikipedia.org/wiki/Las_Trampas,_New_Mexico

On into Taos

N.M. 76 continues up toward the fertile valley of Peñasco. Atop this valley lies the Picuris Indian reservation. At this juncture follow N.M. 518 north towards Taos. Soon you'll be soaking in the magnificence of the Carson National Forest. Look for the Cantonment Burguin, set up after the Taos Revolt (1847) against American forces. The village of Talpa comes right before 518 intersects with N.M. 68. Make a right and continue up towards the town of Taos.

- fs.fed.us/r3/carson

THE LOW ROAD TO TAOS

The "low road" is the highway; take U.S. 84/285 north out of Santa Fe. You'll pass the Santa Fe Opera and the Tesuque Pueblo Flea Market on your left, and you'll be treated to the beauty of the Sangre de Cristo Mountains in a glorious panorama laid out before you.

- sangres.com/sitemap.htm
- en.wikipedia.org/wiki/Sangre_de_Cristo_Mountains

Española and Velarde

Continue through Española, a city even older than Santa Fe, moving onto N.M. 68 (U.S. 84/285 diverges to the left and leads to Abiquiú, yet another country side trip. Soon you will enter Velarde, which, along with Dixon and Embudo, is one of many small villages in this fruit-growing area of the state. People don't think of New Mexicans as fruit producers, but apricots, peaches, apples and raspberries are the main crops in Velarde. The seasonal roadside stands sell many varieties of fruit, jams and *ristras* (wreathes or strands of chile) as well as pottery and other colorful items.

- espanolaonline.com
- en.wikipedia.org/wiki/Espanola,_New_Mexico

Towns along the River

Up the road, you'll pass Embudo Station. During the summer months, a lovely restaurant on the other side of the river specializes in brewed beer and barbecue. Right outside of Embudo you'll see a classic Hispanic country cemetery. Just beyond, at the Rio Grande Gorge Visitors Center, you can stop for information about the route and available activities, mainly river rafting. During spring and summer, the river is filled with rafts and kayaks. Early spring runoff sometimes contains rushing rapids, but later, for the most part, the water is relatively calm, with some rough spots—"The Box," right above Taos, and "The Toilet Bowl," a dangerous whirlpool just below the village of Pilar. If you decide to go river rafting, your guide can help you select the type of experience for you.
embudostation.com/embudo.htm

Winding on up the road, you come to the tiny village of Pilar, where many rafting trips commence. The road is fairly curvy at this point, and, after climbing upward, you finally arrive at a plateau with a view that stretches our forever. From here you can see Mount Wheeler, at 13,161 feet, the highest peak in New Mexico.

- americasroof.com/nm.html

San Francisco de Assisi Village Church
N.M. 68, Ranchos de Taos
(505) 758-2754

Shortly you'll approach Ranchos de Taos, a small village made famous by Georgia O'Keeffe, Ansel Adams, Paul Strand and others who captured with their artistic skills the adobe fortress that is the San Francisco de Assisi Village Church. The back of the church (not the front!) with

San Francisco de Assisi Village Church. The back of the church has been the focus of artists and photographers alike for many years.

its buttresses and undulating adobe has captivated painters and photographers alike. Built in 1815 by the Franciscans, the church is four miles south of Taos on N.M. 68. From here you can continue on into Taos.
  • en.wikipedia.org/wiki/Ranchos_de_Taos,_New_Mexico

Best Food Bet

Before you leave this village, you might opt for lunch or dinner. At the crossroads of Highways 64 and 518, you will see the Trading Post Café. Formerly a general store since before the Great Depression, it was a true community center where you could buy clothing, drugs, fresh and canned food, liquor or soda, and lunch at the counter. Today, it is a wonderful restaurant serving unpretentious, yet sophisticated food in a simple, warm setting.

Trading Post Café
Highway 68 at Highway 518, Ranchos de Taos
(575) 785-5089
tradingpostcafe.com

PLACES TO SEE WHILE IN TAOS

Keep in mind that simply doing the low and high road to Taos and back to Santa Fe can be an all-day excursion, depending on stops. Seeing all that Taos itself has to offer is in itself at least another full day of touring. We do recommend that you take a self-guided walking tour of downtown Taos, availing yourself as well of the art museums both in town and slightly out of town. You can buy a combination ticket for the walking tour or house tour, or a more inclusive ticket that includes the museums.

- taosmuseums.org

Governor Bent House
117-A Bent Street
(505) 758-2376
laplaza.org/art/museums_bent.php3

As a result of the Mexican War in 1846, the United States annexed New Mexico. Charles Bent was then appointed the first Territorial governor. He married Maria Ignacia, the older sister of Josefa Jaramillo, wife of the legendary Kit Carson. Bent, a mountain man, trader and trapper, was killed and scalped in 117-A Bent Street by an angry mob protesting the U.S. annexation, less than a year after his appointment.

Ernest Blumenschein House
222 Ledoux Street
(505) 758-0505
taosmuseums.org/blumenschein.php

In the early 1900s Blumenschein and fellow artist Bert Phillips were touring New Mexico from Chicago. The wheel on their wagon broke, and Bert volunteered to take it into the nearest town for repair. When he returned with the repaired wheel, he told Blumenschein that he had just discovered the ideal town in which to live and paint. These two became the first of the Eastern artists in Taos and were the beginning of the Taos Society of Artists. Dating back to 1797, this house will take you back in time to the peaceful, old Taos days.

The Kit Carson House
One-half block from Taos Plaza on Kit Carson Road
(505) 758-4741
kitcarsonhome.com/kc
en.wikipedia.org/wiki/Kit_Carson

The house in which Kit and his wife, Josefa, lived for 25 years is filled with Indian artifacts and period furniture of the 1800s. Although a general in the Union Army, Kit was illiterate, not unusual in those days. Nonetheless, he had an amazing facility for languages and served as a translator for a wagon train to Chihuahua. A man of many talents, Kit Carson served as a scout for the John C. Fremont expeditions, worked as an Indian agent and thereafter became a military officer. An authentic American hero, he was a Mason in the Santa Fe Masonic Lodge. Though only five foot four inches tall, he had the respect of all he met. During his lifetime many so-called "blood and thunder" books were written about his exploits.

Kit Carson Memorial State Park
Paseo del Pueblo Norte at Civic Plaza
(505) 758-8234

This lovely park is home to many local outdoor events, including the annual Taos Solar Music Festival. It also houses recreational activities and a small cemetery. Buried here are Mabel Dodge Luhan, Padre Antonio José Martinez—who was always at odds with Archbishop Lamy—and, of course, Kit and Josefa Jaramillo Carson.
- Open every day 8 a.m.-8 p.m. in warm weather; 9 a.m.-5 p.m. in the winter

E. I. Couse Home and Studio
146 Kit Carson Road
(505) 751-0369 or (505) 737-0105
cousefoundation.org

E. I. Couse was one of the six founding artists of the Taos Society of Artists. The house, designated a National Trust Associate Site in 2002, stands as a testament to the beginnings of Taos as an American art colony. It houses the original furnishings and Couse's collection of Indian artifacts.
- Open May-October

Harwood Foundation Museum and Library
238 Ledoux Street
(505) 758-9826
harwoodmuseum.org

With its exhibition program and its growing permanent collection, the fascinating Harwood Museum serves as a valuable resource for the Northern New Mexico region. It also provides a research facility for many scholars, educators, authors and students. If you'd like to see more representations of the Taos Society of Artists, then head up the street to the Harwood.

Mabel Dodge Luhan House
Historic Inn and Conference Center
240 Morada Lane
(800) 846-2235 or (505) 751-9686
mabeldodgeluhan.com

During the 1920s wealthy socialite Mabel Dodge Luhan and her husband, Tony, from Taos Pueblo, constructed a large airy home surrounding a small dark adobe building now over 200 years old. Los Gallos, as the home was named, came to represent a conjunction between an elite world of artists and philosophers and one of the most enduring Native societies in the U.S. Guests over the years included Emma Goldman, Alfred Stieglitz, Margaret Sanger, John Reed and others of the political and artistic avant-garde. Other famous visitors included Georgia O'Keeffe, Willa Cather, Ansel Adams and Carl Jung. The late actor Dennis Hopper owned the house briefly in the '70s, and his guests included Bob Dylan, Alan Watts and George McGovern. In 1991 the Mabel Dodge Luhan House was designated a National Historic Landmark and is now open to the public as a bed-and-breakfast, retreat and conference center.

Martinez Hacienda
Off Highway 68 at Ranchos de Taos,
then left on N.M. 240 for 3 miles
(505) 758-1000
taosmuseums.org/hac_martinez.php

Built between 1804 and 1827, this hacienda served as a fortress against Indian raids. Severino Martinez, both trader and farmer, was the builder. Traders using the *Camino Real* (Royal Road) unloaded goods in Santa Fe and then headed to Taos and the Martinez Hacienda, their last stop. Its restored rooms display furniture, crafts and food of the period and will give you genuine insight into life during that time.

Rio Grande Gorge Bridge
From N.M. 68, make a left onto U.S. 64 and
go west to the bridge.
sangres.com/statenm/riogrgorge.htm

We've all seen bridges, but you shouldn't miss this one. Built in 1965, it's the second highest cantilevered bridge in the country and 1,271 feet long. In fact, standing on it and looking into the awesome gorge 650 feet below can bring on vertigo. If you've got the energy, hike down the path into the gorge, or hike at least some of the way down. Make sure you have a hat, sunglasses, plenty of water and, of course, wear hiking boots.

The Millicent Rogers Museum
1504 Museum Road
(505) 758-2462
millicentrogers.com

Millicent Rogers (1902-1953) was the granddaughter of one of the original founders of Standard Oil, Henry Huttleston Rogers. She lived much of her life in Europe but was drawn to the beauty and history of Taos, and she began collecting Indian and Hispanic art and crafts. Her collection, encompassing well over 5,000 pieces, includes María Martínez pottery as well as rugs, blankets, jewelry, *kachinas*, paintings and religious objects. The museum is extraordinary and shows you what can happen when people who have money also have passion and good taste and love collecting. The site itself is breathtaking for its mountain and high desert vistas.

Taos Art Museum at the Fechin House
227 Paseo del Pueblo Norte
(505) 758-2690
taosartmuseum.org
fechin.com

The Russian artist, architect and sculptor Nicolai Fechin lived here from 1927 to 1933. The building is a monument to the architectural marriage of an adobe house and a Russian interpretation of *corbels*, beams and windows. The Taos Art Museum, featuring the works of the Taos Society of Artists, moved to this space in 2003.

Taos Pueblo
Off N.M. 68
(505) 758-1028
taospueblo.com

The Taos Pueblo or "Place of the Red Willows" looks much as it did in the late 1550s when the Spanish arrived. The adobe shape resembles the Taos Mountain directly behind it. It was designated a World Heritage Site in 1992. The original San Geronimo Chapel was built in 1619. The U.S. Army destroyed it in 1850 during the annexation of the New Mexican Territory, but it has since been rebuilt. Traditional and contemporary arts and crafts are sold, as well as bread and traditional foods.

TAOS RESTAURANTS

$ inexpensive: up to $20
$$ moderate: $20 to $35
$$$ expensive: $35 to $55
$$$$ very expensive: $55 or more

Here are a few Taos restaurants that you may want to try. They match our standard of ambience and, in some cases, a sense of history.

Doc Martin's at the Taos Inn
125 Paseo del Pueblo Norte
(888) 518-8278 or (575) 758-1977
taosinn.com/restaurant.html

This historic restaurant, now just over 70 years old, once held the offices of Dr. Thomas Martin. It serves regional, contemporary cuisine. The restaurant and hotel lobby are the social center of the town.
• Serving breakfast, lunch and dinner, $$

Graham's Grille
107 Paseo Del Pueblo Norte
(575) 751-1350
thefayway.com

Leslie B. Fay, one of Taos' best chefs, runs this hip restaurant, specializing in non-fussy food at reasonable prices.
- Serving breakfast, lunch, dinner and weekend brunch, $-$$

Lambert's of Taos
309 Paseo del
Pueblo Sur Taos
(575) 758-1009
lambertsoftaos.com

This restaurant, in a Victorian cottage, is always a best bet for fine dining. The Colorado Rack of Lamb is a standout, but then again that goes for all of the dishes.
- Dinner only, $$-$$$

De La Tierra Restaurant
At El Monte Sagrado
317 Kit Carson Road
(800) 828.8267 or
(575)-758-3502
elmontesagrado.com/dining/de_la_tierra.asp

Within the walls of El Monte Sagrado, a luxury hotel, is de La Tierra Restaurant. It was recently named one of the world's best new restaurants by *Condé Nast Traveler* magazine. This environmentally-conscious resort has a chef who creates seasonal, regional and sustainable cuisine. Of course!
- Serving breakfast, lunch and dinner, $$$-$$$$

11
THE PUEBLOS

Any trip to New Mexico and Santa Fe would hardly be complete without a seeing at least one pueblo in the area. A visit to a pueblo, especially during a feast day when dances take place, is to truly absorb the culture and flavor of ancient times and the Southwest. Feast days are open to the public.

If you wish, you can gamble at one of the many flourishing pueblo casinos. These have been established to raise money for the tribes, and they have provided jobs as well as funds for essential services such as health centers, schools and college scholarships. Some of the casinos have expanded to include nightclub acts and hotels.

In 1973, John Upton Terrell wrote in his book *Pueblos, Gods and Spaniards*:

> . . . the Indians we call Pueblos are not one people. They belong to four distinct stocks. While similarities are clearly recognizable in their respective cultures, actually their traditional spiritual beliefs, tenets, ideologies, and religious symbols differ in many respects. Rather than being inherent, the noticeable similarities are more likely to be adaptations of each other's mores. This development is understandable if one remembers that, after all, these peoples have lived in relatively close association for a very long time.

Pueblo is not an Indian name. It is a Spanish work meaning "town," and it came into common usage as a convenient term to designate natives who dwelt in permanent buildings constituted of stone, timber and adobe.

In the 16th century there were 89 Pueblos. Today, because of disease, slavery and battles, there are only 19 Pueblos left in New Mexico.

The Pueblos can trace their ancestors back to the Mogollon and Anasazi cultures. They have four distinct language groups. They are Azteco-Zuni, Keresan and Tanoan broken into three subgroups, Tiwa, Tewa and Towa.

Visiting a Pueblo, you'll find three distinct architectural elements. First, a mission Catholic church, a plaza where traditional native dances are held and *kivas*, or chambers in the ground where a secret religious ceremonies are held. This almost parallels a layout of a Spanish town, i.e. the church and a plaza.

The Indian Pueblo Cultural Center
2401 Twelfth Street NW
(one block north of I-40), Albuquerque
(505) 843-7270 or (800) 766-4405 outside of New Mexico
indianpueblo.org

A good introduction to the Pueblo Indians is the Indian Pueblo Cultural Center. If you fly into Albuquerque, you can visit before heading north to Santa Fe.

Owned and operated by the nineteen Indian pueblos of New Mexico, the Indian Pueblo Cultural Center showcases to more than 200,000 visitors each year the history and accomplishments of the Pueblo people, from Pre-Columbian to current time. Its central focus is a 10,000-square-foot museum that presents authentic history and artifacts of traditional Pueblo cultures as well as their contemporary art. The permanent exhibit highlights the creativity and adaptation that made possible the survival, diversity and achievements of each of the nineteen Pueblos. Also featured is a small, changing exhibit that highlights the work of living traditional and contemporary artists, usually those who conduct demonstrations at the center.

Traditional dances and festivals that form the centerpiece of Pueblo Indian spiritual and cultural life are performed in the courtyard. Performers from the nineteen New Mexico pueblos, from other Indian tribes and from other parts of the world are all drawn to the center, where they dance and represent a unique opportunity for visitors to see cultural diversity at one place. Dances are often impromptu affairs and can prove an exciting surprise to the unsuspecting visitor. They are scheduled regularly twice a day on Saturdays and Sundays.

- Open daily 9:00 a.m.-5:30 p.m.
- Museum hours: 9:00 a.m.-4:30 p.m.
- Gift shop hours: 9:00 a.m.-5:30 p.m.
- Pueblo restaurant: 8:00 a.m.-3:00 p.m.
- Discount Pueblo smoke shop: 7 a.m.-6:30 p.m.
- Indian Pueblo Cultural Center admission: free
- Museum admission: $6 per person, seniors $5.50, students $1, children 8 and up $1 and under 7 free with adult.

Pueblos and Spirituality

The pueblos are not only fascinating for their art and their history, but they are mythical places to many people. A case in point is the experience of C. G. Jung, the psychoanalyst, whose thinking transformed modern psychology and who was greatly influenced by a visit to Taos Pueblo.

In 1925, Jung spent time at Taos Pueblo and met Taos elder Ochwiay Biano (Mountain Lake). The perceptions Jung came away with from this meeting made a powerful impression on him and helped frame his conception of the psyche. He also witnessed how the Taos people retained age-old sacred rituals, which they kept secret to themselves and which gave them a connection with the mythic, archetypical, spiritual world. Jung wrote in his autobiography, *Memories, Dreams, Reflections*, "Preservation of secret traditions gives the Pueblo Indian pride and the power to resist the dominant whites. It gives them cohesion and unity; and I feel sure that the Pueblos as individual communities will continue to exist as long as their mysteries are not desecrated." (Jung, p. 250)

Jung also quoted Mountain Lake in his book, "We are a people who live on the roof of the world; we are the sons of Father Sun, and with our religion we daily help our father to go across the sky. We do this not only for ourselves, but for the whole world." (Jung, p. 252)

- en.wikipedia.org/wiki/Pueblo_people
- puebloindian.com
- eightnorthernpueblos.com
- indianpueblo.org

Pueblo Etiquette

When visiting foreign countries it's appropriate to observe their rules and customs. The same courtesies apply when you visit the pueblos of Northern New Mexico. Some pueblos have fees for admission and for photography. In most instances, photography of dances and feast-day celebrations is prohibited. Some activities are closed to the public, and this needs to be respected. Here is a list to use as a guide:

- Please observe all rules and regulations of the individual pueblos.
- All homes at each pueblo are private. Never enter without an invitation.
- Please guide your children and see that they are respectful.
- Climbing walls or other structures is not permitted. Remember that some walls are several hundred years old and could be easily damaged.
- Removing any artifacts or objects, such as pieces of broken pottery, is forbidden.
- Please do not enter any *kivas* or graveyards.
- Alcohol, weapons and drugs are not tolerated.
- No pets are allowed.
- All Pueblo dances are religious ceremonies, not staged performances, and must be attended with respect.
- During the dances, please do not interrupt non-dancers' concentration by talking or waving to friends.
- Please do not talk to the dancers.
- No applause after dances, please.

Visiting a Pueblo Home

Entering a pueblo home is by invitation only. It is polite to accept an invitation to eat, but do not linger at the table as your host will be serving many guests throughout the day. Extend your thanks, but know that a payment is not appropriate.

Photography

Please contact each pueblo regarding permits, fees and restrictions concerning photography. Photographs are for your private use only. Ask permission before taking someone's photograph.

Which Pueblo Should I Visit?

This book was designed to appeal to the visitor with limited time. There are nineteen pueblos across Northern New Mexico—more pueblos than you'll have time to explore. Eight of these pueblos are within easy driving distance of Santa Fe, with a drive time of between 30 minutes to 1-1/2 hours drive time (Taos, combine with trip to Taos). We suggest that you check out the feast days and choose to visit those pueblos that mesh with your schedule in Santa Fe.

Eight Northern Indian Pueblos

Located north of Santa Fe, these pueblos have for years been working together to create economic opportunities that benefit both themselves and the surrounding communities. Every summer, they put on one of the finest Indian arts and crafts shows in the country, the Eight Northern Indian Pueblos Council Artists and Craftsmen Show. The show is held the third week of July at the Eight Northern Indian Pueblos Indian Arts and Crafts Center at San Juan Pueblo. This is a wonderful opportunity for you to visit a pueblo and purchase some of the finest Indian arts and crafts directly from the artists at prices considerably lower than retail. For details on this year's show, call (505) 747-1593, extension 112, or visit their website.

- eightnorthernpueblos.com

Nambé Pueblo
(505) 455-2036
Distance from Santa Fe: 17 miles

Nambé Pueblo is 12 miles north of Santa Fe on U.S. 84/285. Just after Pojoaque, turn right on N.M. 503. The pueblo is about four miles off N.M. 503, down a side road.

The best time to visit this small pueblo is on its major feast day, October 4, celebrating the Vespers of St. Francis of Assisi Day. Also of interest are the Nambé waterfalls and a lake that supplies water for the surrounding farmland.

- nmmagazine.com/NMGUIDE/nambe.html
- indianpueblo.org/ipcc/nambepage.htm
- en.wikipedia.org/wiki/Nambe_Pueblo

Picuris Pueblo
(505) 587-2519

Distance from Santa Fe: 60 miles. Go north on U.S. 84/285 from Santa Fe, then take N.M. 68 out of Española. At Embudo, turn onto N.M. 75.

Picuris is the smallest, most highly elevated (7,324 feet) and the most physically isolated of the nineteen pueblos. The Picuris Indians are the majority owners of one of Santa Fe's finest hotels—the Hotel Santa Fe—that status offering a viable future income to the residents of the pueblo.

The feast day on August 10 commemorates the Pueblo Revolt against Spanish occupation, which occurred on August 10, 1680.
- picurispueblo.net
- nmmagazine.com/NMGUIDE/picuris.html
- indianpueblo.org/ipcc/picurispage.htm
- en.wikipedia.org/wiki/Picuris_Pueblo,_New_Mexico
- hotelsantafe.com

Pojoaque Pueblo
(505) 455-2278

Pojoaque Pueblo is 15 miles north of Santa Fe just off U.S. 84/285.

The original name of this Pueblo is Po-suwae-geh, or "water drinking place." In fact, the pueblo was a place for travelers to stop and shop.

The main attraction here is the Poeh Cultural Center and Museum, which also has a gift shop and artist studios. The feast day, December 12, celebrates Our Lady of Guadalupe. Near the pueblo you'll find the Cities of Gold Casino.
- en.wikipedia.org/wiki/Pojoaque_Pueblo
- citiesofgold.com
- poehcenter.com

San Ildefonso Pueblo
(505) 455-2273

Take U.S. 84/25 north. Just after passing Pojoaque, pick up N.M. 502 heading towards Los Alamos. Continue for 7 miles to the San Ildefonso turnoff. Distance from Santa Fe is 25 miles.

One cannot visit this pueblo without feeling the presence of María Martínez and her son Julian, who developed the "black on black" pottery in 1919. To own a "Maria pot" is to own something beautiful and quite valuable. It is therefore not unusual that many of the inhabitants of this pueblo are potters and have been so for many generations. In addition, San Ildefonso has artisans who specialize in paintings, silver jewelry, embroidery and moccasins. The pueblo feast day is January 23, when Comanche, Buffalo and Deer Dances are held.

- en.wikipedia.org/wiki/San_Ildefonso_Pueblo

Ohkay Owingeh (formerly San Juan Pueblo)
(505) 852-4400

Take U.S. 84/285 north. When you arrive in Española, follow the signs to stay on highway 285. Distance from Santa Fe is 36 miles.

Historically, this pueblo is most interesting. Don Juan de Oñate, a Spanish colonizer, came here from Mexico in 1598 with plans to erect a major city. This pueblo was, in fact, the predecessor of Santa Fe and was renamed San Juan de los Caballeros to replace the Indian name, Ohkay Owingeh, which the Pueblo has recently restored.

The Ohkay Owingeh feast day is held on June 24 to honor St. John the Baptist, the patron saint of the pueblo. Buffalo and Comanche dances are held on the feast days.

The pueblo operates one of the largest casinos in New Mexico, the Best Western Ohkay Casino-Resort and holds the Eight Northern Indian Pueblos Council Artists and Craftsmen Show every July.

- en.wikipedia.org/wiki/Ohkay_Owingeh_Pueblo
- eightnorthernpueblos.com
- casinocity.com/us/nm/sanjuanpueblo/ohkay

Santa Clara Pueblo
(505) 753-7326

Take U.S. 84/285 north. In Española, take N.M. 201, and then go one mile southwest on N.M. 30. Distance from Santa Fe is 34 miles.

The people of Santa Clara can trace their ancestry to the occupants of a cliffside village known as the Puye Cliff Dwellings. The stunning ruins were built alongside a cliff face in the Santa Clara Canyon and are open to

One of the many caves, carved out of volcanic ash, at the Puye Cliff Dwellings, the original home of the Santa Clara people for over 400 years.

visitors year round. In the 1500s, severe drought forced them to move into the valley of the Rio Grande, where the pueblo thrives today. Pottery is their main craft, and they are famous for their highly polished Blackware and Redware hand-coiled pots.

There are two feast days—June 13 and August 12—the "Big Feast" where Harvest, Blue Corn and other dances are performed. Santa Clara Pueblo owns the Black Mesa Golf Club, and it operates a casino and bowling alley, Big Rock Casino, in the middle of Española.

- en.wikipedia.org/wiki/Santa_Clara_Pueblo
- blackmesagolfclub.com
- bigrockcasino.com

Taos Pueblo
(575) 758-1028

Take U.S. 84/285 north, then N.M. 68. Go straight through the town of Taos. The Pueblo is 2.7 miles north of Taos itself. Distance from Santa Fe is 65 miles.

Taos Pueblo, or "the Place of the Red Willows," sells both traditional and contemporary arts and crafts. Oven bread and traditional foods are also available.

The old Taos Pueblo graveyard is no longer used.

The pueblo is open to tourists daily from 9 a.m. to 5 p.m., with fees for visiting and photographing. The feast days are May 3 (traditional foot races and Corn Dances); June 13, July 25 and 26 (Santiago's Day); September 30 (The Feast of San Geronimo). Taos also has a casino, Taos Mountain Casino.

- taospueblo.com
- en.wikipedia.org/wiki/Taos_Pueblo
- taosmountaincasino.com

Tesuque Pueblo
(505) 983-2667

Take U.S. 84/285 north. Turn right at the sign for Tesuque. Distance from Santa Fe is 9 miles.

The original pueblo existed before the year 1200, east of the current village. The current pueblo was reestablished in 1694, soon after the Pueblo Revolt of 1680.

The annual feast day at the pueblo is on November 12 and commemorates San Diego. There is also a Corn Dance in June. Pueblo artists are in abundance, and many will sell artwork from their homes.

Acoma Pueblo is the oldest continuously inhabited city in the United States.

The casino here is Camel Rock. The pueblo also runs the Tesuque Pueblo Flea Market.
- en.wikipedia.org/wiki/Tesuque,_New_Mexico
- camelrockcasino.com

Pueblos South of Santa Fe

In addition to the eight northern pueblos, there are eleven pueblos south of Santa Fe. All are quite interesting, so I'll leave it up to you. One mitigating factor is the amount of time you have in Santa Fe. Of course, there's always another visit to New Mexico, or if you have come to Santa Fe by way of Albuquerque, you will find several on your way back or just slightly out of the way once there.

Acoma Pueblo
(505) 552-6604

Take I-25 south, then drive west from Albuquerque on I-40 (60 miles) and then 12 miles south on Indian Route 23 (exit 108). Distance from Santa Fe is 132 miles.

Acoma, one of the most famous pueblos, is the oldest continuously inhabited city in the United States. It was built on top of a 357-foot sandstone mesa for defensive purposes over a thousand years ago. In a pitched battle against the Spanish troops of Juan de Oñate, the pueblo was nearly destroyed. Later, in a spiritually related conciliatory gesture, the Spanish mission of San Esteban del Rey Mission was built and completed in 1640. Guided tours are available. The pueblo also runs the Sky City Casino.

- en.wikipedia.org/wiki/Acoma_Pueblo
- skycitycasino.com

Cochiti Pueblo
(505) 465-2244

Take I-25 south for 22 miles. Exit at N.M. 26 and go another 14 miles. Distance from Santa Fe is 27 miles.

The inhabitants of Cochiti Pueblo are famous for their handmade ceremonial drums as well as the storyteller ceramic figures originally created by the late Helen Cordero. These figures are now world-famous. You can also swim and boat at Cochiti Lake, where summer events are periodically held, or play golf at the 18-hole championship course nearby.

- en.wikipedia.org/wiki/Cochiti,_New_Mexico

Isleta Pueblo
(505) 869-3111

Take I-25 south to Albuquerque and turn right off Exit 215. Distance from Santa Fe is 73 miles.

Isleta, "little island" in Spanish, was established in the 1300s. St. Augustine Church, built in 1612 and located on the main plaza, is fascinating historically and boasts traditional architecture. The pueblo operates the Isleta Casino and Resort, one of the largest pueblo casinos.

- isletapueblo.com
- en.wikipedia.org/wiki/Isleta_Pueblo
- isletacasinoresort.com

Jemez Pueblo
(505) 834-7235

Take I-25 south to the Cuba exit and continue for 27 miles on U.S. 550. Distance from Santa Fe is 67 miles.

Jemez combined with the Pecos Pueblo in 1838, when the people from the Pueblo of Pecos (located east of Santa Fe) resettled at the Pueblo of Jemez in order to escape the increasing depredations of the Spanish and Comanche cultures. They were rapidly integrated into Jemez society, and in 1936, both cultural groups were legally merged into one by an act of Congress. Today, the Pecos culture still survives at Jemez. The pueblo village, Walatowa, is only open to visitors on feast days, so call ahead for feast-day dates. Their visitor center, however, is always open and displays a reconstructed Jemez field house and other cultural exhibits as well as a gift shop.

- jemezpueblo.org
- en.wikipedia.org/wiki/Jemez_Pueblo,_New_Mexico

Kewa Pueblo (formerly Santo Domingo)
(505) 465-2214

Take I-25 south to the Santo Domingo exit and turn west. The pueblo is halfway between Santa Fe and Albuquerque. Distance from Santa Fe is 25 miles.

Kewa Pueblo is located close to the old Cerrillos Hills turquoise mines. Is it any wonder that Kewa Indians are skilled in the art of turquoise and *heishi* jewelry? The big annual event at the pueblo is the arts-and-crafts show held each Labor Day, but roadside stands selling jewelry as well as pottery are to be found in the pueblo year round. August 4 is the Feast of St. Dominic. This is the largest feast-day dance of all the pueblos, with thousands doing the traditional Corn Dance.

- en.wikipedia.org/wiki/Santo_Domingo_Pueblo,_New_Mexico

Laguna Pueblo
(505) 552-6654

Take I-25 south to Albuquerque, take I-40 west for 45 miles. The pueblo is 31 miles east of Grants. Distance from Santa Fe is 105 miles.

Laguna Pueblo was named after a lake that has since disappeared from the area. The Pueblo and its famous mission church—San José de Laguna—were founded in 1699 by refugees from Cochiti and Kewa (Santo Domingo) at the end of the Pueblo Revolt. It has a population of about 7,700, making it one of the largest Keresan pueblos.

Pottery and other crafts are for sale all year, but the September 19 Feast of St. Joseph generally has hundreds of booths with crafts for sale. The pueblo operates the Dancing Eagle Casino, located on N.M. 114.

- en.wikipedia.org/wiki/Laguna_Pueblo
- dancingeaglecasino.com

Sandia Pueblo
(505) 867-3317

Take I-25 south to west on Exit 235 and then about 12 miles to the Pueblo. Distance from Santa Fe is 62 miles.

This pueblo goes back to the 1300s. Originally named Nafiat ("dusty") it was given its modern name Sandia ("watermelon") by later Spanish colonists, who saw what they thought were watermelons growing in the pueblo. The Sandia Mountains were named after the pueblo. A large pueblo, it operates one of the biggest Native-owned arts-and-crafts markets in the Southwest, Bien Mur Indian Market, as well as one of the largest casinos, Sandia Resort and Casino. Both are located on the east side of I-25 off Tramway Boulevard.

- sandiapueblo.nsn.us
- en.wikipedia.org/wiki/Sandia_Pueblo
- bienmur.com
- sandiacasino.com

San Felipe Pueblo
(505) 867-3381

Take I-25 south for 40 miles to the San Felipe Pueblo exit.

One of the most conservative of the pueblos, San Felipe was founded in the 1300s. The yearly highlight of the village is the celebration of the Feast of St. Philip on May 1. Then, hundreds of villagers do the beautiful and relentless Corn Dance. Crafts and jewelry are sold, especially during the arts-and-crafts show in October. Additionally, the tribe owns and operates the Casino Hollywood right off I-25, as well as the Hollywood Hills Speedway, where racing, outdoor events and concerts are held.

- en.wikipedia.org/wiki/San_Felipe_Pueblo,_New_Mexico
- sanfelipecasino.com

Santa Ana Pueblo
(505) 867-3301

Take I-25 south to Exit 242 and drive 2 miles west to the intersection of U.S. 550 and N.M. 528 (Dove Road). Turn right (north) to entrance of resort on right. Distance from Santa Fe is 45 miles.

The Santa Ana Pueblo people have occupied their current site in central New Mexico since at least the late 1500s. The original pueblo, at approximately 5,400 feet above sea level, lies against a mesa wall on the north bank of the Jemez River, a site providing protection and seclusion. For the most part travelers followed the north-south trade route along the Rio Grande or headed east and west; they made little contact, and as a result Santa Ana was seldom visited.

The pueblo is only open to the public on feast days (January 1 and 6, as well as July 26, Santiago's Day).

The pueblo operates the Santa Ana and Twin Warriors Golf Clubs, the Santa Ana Garden Center, the highly prosperous Santa Ana Star Casino, and the luxurious Hyatt Regency Tamaya Resort and Spa.
- santaana.org
- en.wikipedia.org/wiki/Santa_Ana_Pueblo,_New_Mexico
- santaanagolf.com/Santa_Ana
- twinwarriorsgolf.com
- tamaya.hyatt.com/property/index.jhtml
- santaanastar.com

Zia Pueblo
(505) 867-3304

Take I-25 south to U.S. 550 west for about 25 miles to the pueblo. Distance from Santa Fe is 65 miles.

This Keres-speaking pueblo is widely known for its ancient sun symbol and the thin-walled, Zia bird-symbol pottery. The sun symbol graphically depicts multiple stylized rays radiating in each of the four directions from a central sun. This symbol has been on the New Mexico flag since the 1920s. If you fly over the state Capitol in Santa Fe, you will see that the roof has a depiction of the sun symbol.

The Zia Cultural Center has pottery, sculpture and weavings for sale.

The Feast Day honoring Our Lady of the Assumption takes place on August 15.
- zia.com/home/Zia_Info.html
- en.wikipedia.org/wiki/Zia_Pueblo,_New_Mexico
- nmsu.edu/~bho/zia.html

Zuni Pueblo
(505) 782-4403

Take I-25 south to Albuquerque and take I-40 west. Look for the Zuni Pueblo exit (N.M. 55), 35 miles before Gallup. Distance from Santa Fe is 180 miles.

Coronado, in his quest for gold, thought he had come upon one of the Seven Cities of Cibola when he entered the Zuni Pueblo. He found no gold, but today a visitor will find an abundance of turquoise and silver jewelry, including needlepoint and inlay jewelry. The Zuni are the main carvers of fetishes—various stones carved into the likenesses of animals. Originally carved for hunters for protection and successful hunts, they are widely sought out by collectors around the world. Keshi, a store at 227 Don Gasper Avenue in Santa Fe, has had close ties with the pueblo since 1981, when it became a co-op for these beautiful carvings and other crafts.

Zuni is the most populated of all the pueblos. Its mission church, Our Lady of Guadalupe, built in 1629, contains some ten-foot *kachina* murals painted by Alex Seowtewa. Call ahead for hours.
- ashiwi.org
- experiencezuni.com
- en.wikipedia.org/wiki/Zuni_Pueblo,_New_Mexico
- keshi.com

Our thanks to the New Mexico Department of Tourism for helping us to compile this section.

PUEBLO CASINOS (Subject to change)

Big Rock Casino Bowl
(505) 753-7326

Santa Clara Pueblo, distance from Santa Fe is 34 miles. Big Rock Casino Bowl includes bowling alley.
- bigrockcasino.com

Buffalo Thunder Resort and Casino
(505) 455-5555

Pojoaque Pueblo, distance from Santa Fe is 15 miles.

Buffalo Thunder and Hilton Hotel is the largest hotel in New Mexico with 395 rooms, 5 restaurants, a Las Vegas style casino, an outstanding collection of Native American art and sculpture, and 36-hole golf course.
- buffalothunderresort.com

Camel Rock Casino
(505) 983-2667

Tesuque Pueblo, distance from Santa Fe is 9 miles. Camel Rock Casino, Camel Rock Suites Hotel and The Rock Showroom featuring national music acts and boxing.
- camelrockcasino.com

Cities of Gold Casino
(505) 455-2278

Pojoaque Pueblo, distance from Santa Fe is 15 miles.

Cities of Gold Casino, with sports bar featuring simulcast wagering, Towa Golf Course, Cities of Gold Hotel and full-service restaurant, Golden Cantina for drinks and live music.
- citiesofgold.com

Dancing Eagle Casino
(505) 552-6654

Laguna Pueblo, distance from Santa Fe is 105 miles.
Dancing Eagle Casino, with restaurant and snack bar.
- dancingeaglecasino.com

Isleta Casino and Resort
(505) 869-3111

Isleta Pueblo, distance from Santa Fe is 73 miles.
Isleta Casino and Resort, several restaurants, national big-name music acts, Isleta Eagle 27-hole championship golf course.
- isletacasinoresort.com

Ohkay Casino-Resort
(505) 869-3111

Ohkay Owingeh (formerly San Juan Pueblo), distance from Santa Fe is 26 miles.

Ohkay Casino-Resort, Best Western hotel, Ohkay Corral, 1,500-seat venue for rodeos and outdoor events and concerts.

- casinocity.com/us/nm/sanjuanpueblo/ohkay

San Felipe Casino Hollywood
(505) 867-3381

San Felipe Pueblo, distance from Santa Fe is 40 miles.

San Felipe Casino Hollywood with Celebrity Showroom featuring national music acts and Hollywood Hills Speedway, where auto racing, outdoor events and concerts are held.

- sanfelipecasino.com

Sandia Casino
(505) 867-3317

Sandia Pueblo, distance from Santa Fe is 62 miles.

Sandia Casino with buffet dining.

- sandiacasino.com

Santa Ana Star Casino
(505) 867-3001

Santa Ana Pueblo, distance from Santa Fe is 45 miles.

Santa Ana Star Casino, 3,000-seat arena with national acts, 45-hole championship golf (Twin Warriors and Santa Ana Golf), Starlight Lanes bowling, arcade games.

- santaanastar.com

Sky City Casino
(505) 552-6017

Acoma Pueblo, distance from Santa Fe is 132 miles.

Sky City Casino, Huwaka Restaurant, Sky City Hotel and Conference Center.

- skycitycasino.com

Taos Mountain Casino
(575) 758-1028

Taos Pueblo, distance from Santa Fe is 65 miles.

Taos Mountain Casino, featuring majestic views and live local music.

- taosmountaincasino.com

CALENDAR OF DANCES & FEAST DAYS

Please call prior to visiting any pueblo for changes and updates on events.

- indianpueblo.org (then follow prompts to calendar)
- santaana.org/calendar.htm

January 1

- Taos Pueblo—Turtle Dance
- Kewa Pueblo—Corn Dance
- Ohkay Owingeh (San Juan) Pueblo—Cloud or Basket Dance

January 6—Kings Day Celebration
(annual transference of leadership)

- Most pueblos have dances on Jan. 6th
- Picuris Pueblo—various dances
- Nambé Pueblo—Buffalo, Deer and Antelope Dances
- Sandia Pueblo—Various Dances
- Taos Pueblo—Deer or Buffalo Dances

January 22

- San Ildefonso Pueblo—Vespers Evening with firelight procession 6 p.m.—call to confirm.

January 23

- San Ildefonso Pueblo—Annual Feast Day—Buffalo, Comanche & Deer Dances

January 25

- Picuris Pueblo—St. Paul's Feast Day—Various Dances

February—1st weekend

- Old Acoma Pueblo—Governor's Feast Day—Various Dances

February 2

- San Felipe and Picuris Pueblos—Candelaria Day Celebration

March 19—St. Joseph's Feast Day

- Old Laguna Pueblo—Harvest Dance & Various Dances

Easter Weekend

- At most Pueblos—Basket and Corn Dances
- Nambé Pueblo—Bow & Arrow Dance after Mass
- Zia Pueblo—Various Dances
- San Ildefonso—Various Dances

April 22-24

- Gathering of Nations Pow Wow in Albuquerque
- gatheringofnations.com/

May 1

- San Felipe Pueblo—St. Philip Feast day—Corn Dance

May 3

- Taos Pueblo—Corn Dance—Santa Cruz Feast Day—Blessing of the Fields

May—Memorial Day Weekend

- Jemez Pueblo—Annual Red Rocks Arts & Crafts Show

June 13

- Sandia Pueblo—St. Anthony Feast Day—Annual Feast Day
- Taos, San Ildefonso and Picuris Pueblos
- Ohkay Owingeh (San Juan) Pueblo—Green Corn Dances
- Santa Clara Pueblo—Comanche Dance
- Picuris Pueblo—Foot Races

June—Father's Day Weekend

- Picuris Pueblo—Weekend High Country Arts & Crafts Festival

June 24

- Ohkay Owingeh (San Juan) Pueblo—Annual St. John Feast Day—Corn Dances
- Taos Pueblo—Traditional Corn Dances

June 29

- Santa Ana Pueblo—St. Peter's Feast Day—Corn Dance

July—First Weekend

- Picuris Pueblo—Arts & Crafts Fair

July 4

- Nambé Pueblo—Celebration of the waterfall—call to confirm
- Mescalero Apache—Maiden's Puberty Rites and Mountain Spirits Dance

July—Second Weekend

- Taos Pueblo—Annual Intertribal Pow Wow

July 14

- Cochiti Pueblo—St. Bonaventure Feast Day—Corn Dances

Mid-July

- Jicarilla Apache—Little Beaver Roundup and Rodeo and Various Dances in Dulce
- Ohkay Owingeh (San Juan) Pueblo—34th Eight Northern Indian Pueblos Annual Arts & Crafts Fair
- (505) 852-4265 or 800-793-4955
- eightnorthernpueblos.com

July 25

- Taos and other pueblos—Santiago Feast Day—Corn Dances

July 26

- Santa Ana Pueblo—Annual Feast Day—Corn Dance
- Laguna Pueblo—St. Ann's Feast Day—Harvest and various dances
- Taos Pueblo—Corn Dance

Early to Mid August

- Annual International Spiritual Gathering—Rocksprings. Spiritual prayers, Pow Wow, traditional Navajo song and dance, arts & crafts and more. Free Admission.
- (505) 722-2177
- Gallup Inter-tribal Indian Ceremonial: Various dances, parades, arts and crafts and rodeo at Red Rock State Park near Gallup.
- (505) 864-3896
- gallupintertribal.com

August 4

- Kewa Pueblo—Annual Feast Day—Corn Dance

August—Second Weekend

- Zuni Pueblo—Annual Arts and Cultural Expo

August 9

- Picuris Pueblo—San Lorenzo Sunset Dances

August 10—Historical Anniversary Date of Pueblo Revolt

- Acoma Pueblo (Acomita)—San Lorenzo Feast Day
- Picuris Pueblo—Ceremonial foot race, pole climb and dances

August 12

- Santa Clara Pueblo—Annual Feast Day—Buffalo, Harvest or Corn Dance

August 15

- Zia Pueblo—Annual Feast Day—Corn Dances
- Laguna Pueblo—The Assumption of Our Blessed Mother's Feast Day—harvest and various dances at Mesita village

Late August

- Zuni Pueblo—Annual Zuni Tribal Fair

Weekend following the third Thursday in August

- Southwest American Indian Art (SWAIA) Annual Indian Market in Santa Fe
- swaia.org/indianmrkt.html

August 28

- Isleta Pueblo—St. Augustine Feast Day—Mass in the morning and a procession following Mass—Dances in the afternoon

September 2

- Old Acoma Pueblo—Annual San Estevan Feast Day—Harvest Dance

September—First Week

- Annual Navajo Nation Fair
- (928) 871-6478
- navajonationparks.org/

September 4

- Isleta Pueblo—Saint Augustine's Feast Day—Harvest Dance

September—First Weekend

- Kewa Pueblo—Annual Arts & Crafts Show

September 8—Nativity of the Blessed Virgin Mary's Feast Day

- Laguna Pueblo (Encinal village)—Social Dances
- San Ildefonso Pueblo—Corn Dance

September—Second or Third weekend

- Jicarilla Apache—Stone Lake Fiesta—Various dances in Dulce
- (505) 759-3242

September 19

- Old Laguna Pueblo—St. Joseph's Feast Day—Buffalo, Eagle and social dances

September 25

- Laguna Pueblo (Paguate Village)—St. Elizabeth's Feast Day—Harvest and social dances

September 29

- Taos Pueblo—San Geronimo Eve—Vespers—Sunset Dance

September 30

- Taos Pueblo—San Geronimo's Feast Day—Trade fair, ceremonial foot races and pole climb

Early October

- Zuni Pueblo—Zuni Harvest Festival
- (505) 782-4481

October 3

- Nambé Pueblo—Evening Firelight Vespers

October 4

- Nambé Pueblo—St. Francis de Assisi Annual Feast Day—Buffalo and Deer Dances

October 10-11

- Alamo (Navajo) Indian Day
- 854-2686/2688

October 17

- Laguna Pueblo (Paraje Village)—St. Margaret's Feast Day—Harvest and social dances

November 12

- Tesuque Pueblo—San Diego Annual Feast Day—Various dances

November—Last Week

- Zuni Pueblo—Christmas Light Parade

December—First Weekend

- Ohkay Owingeh (San Juan) Pueblo—Eight Northern Indian Pueblos Winter Arts & Crafts Fair

December 11

- Pojoaque Pueblo—Vespers and procession are usually held at 6 p.m.

December 12

- Pojoaque Pueblo—Annual Feast Day—Mass at 10 a.m.—dances performed after the mass.

December 24 and 25

- Picuris Pueblo—Christmas Celebration—Spanish dance drama *Los Matachines*

- Ohkay Owingeh (San Juan) Pueblo—Christmas Celebration—Spanish dance drama *Los Matachines*—Pine Torch Procession

December 24—Christmas Eve

- Taos Pueblo—Sundown procession with bonfires—Children's Dance
- Old Acoma Pueblo—Pueblo is lit with *luminarias* beginning at the Scenic View Point and continues as far as "Sky City"
- Laguna Pueblo—Dances follow 10 a.m. Mass
- San Felipe, Santa Ana & Tesuque Pueblos—Dances after midnight Mass
- Nambé Pueblo—Buffalo Dances after Mass

December 25—Christmas Day

- Tesuque Pueblo—Various dances
- Taos Pueblo—Dances to be announced (Deer or *Los Matachines*)
- San Ildefonso Pueblo—Christmas Celebration—*Los Matachines* Dance

December 26

- Ohkay Owingeh (San Juan) Pueblo—Turtle Dance (no pictures)

December 28

- Santa Clara Pueblo—Innocents Day Dance
- Picuris Pueblo—Holy Innocence Day "Children's Dance"

LA TRIVIATA

© Joel Stein

The Merriam-Webster Dictionary defines trivia as "unimportant matters, obscure facts or details." I, for one, love trivia because these obscure facts bring subject matter to life and give them the ". . . I didn't know that" response.

Because we live in Santa Fe where the opera is such a big part of our cultural life, I have christened our trivia "La Triviata" in homage to the opera *La Traviata*. Enjoy reading them!

⬦⬦⬦

Santa Fe is not named for a saint, but you're in the right "realm." The name "Santa Fe" is Spanish and means "Holy Faith." It was settled by the Spanish in 1610. Don Pedro de Peralta of Spain made Santa Fe the administrative capital of the area. It is the oldest capital in the United States. In the early days, the town was known as *La Villa Real de La Santa Fe de San Francisco de Asis*, "The Royal City of Santa Fe of St. Francis of Assisi." Don Pedro de Peralta became the third of sixty governors of this Spanish colony.

⬦⬦⬦

In 1540 Vásquez de Coronado led an expedition from Mexico into Nueva España looking for gold, especially the Seven Cities of Cibola that were supposedly made of gold. They were really the Zuni Pueblo homes and not golden. The first European to see the Grand Canyon was Garcia Lopez de Cardenas, who was part of the Coronado Expedition.

⬦⬦⬦

In 1550 Charles V of Spain, the most powerful ruler in all of Europe, decreed that no further expeditions be sent into Indian territories until it can be determined that colonization will not do injustice to native inhabitants. Because of this there was no colonization for many years.

∞∞∞

In 1598 the road taken by Juan de Oñate's expedition became known as *El Camino Real* (The Royal Road). It extended nearly 2,000 miles from Mexico City, the longest road in North America for several centuries.

∞∞∞

When Diego de Vargas entered Santa Fe on September 11, 1692, to retake Santa Fe for Spain. He carried Nuestra Señora del Rosario, Our Lady of the Rosary, now popularly known as La Conquistadora.

∞∞∞

In 1757 there were 5,170 Spaniards living in New Mexico and about 9,000 Pueblo and Hopi Indians.

∞∞∞

The Santa Fe Trail, started in 1821, originally ran from Old Franklin, Missouri, to Santa Fe.

∞∞∞

In 1832 a huge adobe structure known as Bent's Fort was completed on the north bank of the Arkansas River near the mouth of the Purgatory River. William Bent managed the fort. Charles Bent brought supplies from Missouri.

∞∞∞

In 1841 John C. Fremont, "The Pathfinder," was married to Jesse Benton, the daughter of Senator Thomas Hart Benton. He was the great uncle of Thomas Hart Benton, the famous American painter of the same name, and also was the greatest exponent of U.S. Westward Expansion, or "Manifest Destiny," proposed by President James Polk., our eleventh president.

∞∞∞

In 1842 Kit Carson was baptized into the Catholic faith by Padre Antonio Martinez of Taos so that he could marry Josefa Jaramillo, the 15-year-old sister of Ignacia Bent, wife of Charles Bent. In 1856 Colonel Kit Carson was a Mason and a member of the Masonic Lodge in Santa Fe, the oldest lodge in New Mexico.

∞∞∞

The Treaty of Guadalupe Hidalgo signed in 1848 with Mexico gave the United States New Mexico, Arizona, Utah, Nevada, California and parts of Colorado and Wyoming. The price—$15 million.

∞∞∞

In 1850 the Sisters of Loretto founded a girls school in Santa Fe, which served New Mexicans until 1969. The site of the school is where the Inn of Loretto now stands.

⬦⬦⬦⬦

Santa Fe has also been home to the notorious, including the famous outlaw Billy the Kid. It is even rumored that he washed dishes and played the piano at La Fonda (the Exchange Hotel at that time), but he didn't even know how to play the piano! Billy the Kid spoke fluent Spanish and was well liked among Spanish people.

⬦⬦⬦⬦

General Lew Wallace, a New Mexico territorial governor in 1879, wrote part of his novel, *Ben Hur*, while residing in the Palace of the Governors in Santa Fe. The museum still has the chair he sat upon while writing. First published in 1880, this book was made into a movie in 1959 starring Charlton Heston. Wallace's frustration in getting things accomplished as governor of the state is summarized by his statement ". . . every calculation based on experience elsewhere, fails in New Mexico."

⬦⬦⬦⬦

The province that was once Spanish New Mexico included all of present-day New Mexico, most of Colorado and Arizona, and slices of Utah, Texas, Oklahoma, Kansas and Wyoming. The original American territory of New Mexico created by Congress in 1850 included all of New Mexico and Arizona plus parts of Colorado, Nevada, and Utah. The boundaries of present-day New Mexico were drawn by Congress in 1863, but New Mexico didn't become the 47th state until January 6, 1912, when President William Howard Taft signed the proclamation. When New Mexicans voted in their first presidential election in 1912, they voted for Woodrow Wilson over Taft.

Miscellaneous Triviata

Georgia O'Keeffe first visited New Mexico in the summer of 1917 and bought her first New Mexico house at Ghost Ranch in October 1940. O'Keeffe moved to Santa Fe in 1984 with her assistant Juan Hamilton and his family. She died at 98 years old in March of 1986 at St. Vincent Hospital in Santa Fe.

⬦⬦⬦⬦

The Santa Fe area is and was the home of many celebrities such as novelists Willa Cather, Tony Hillerman, D. H. Lawrence; artists Georgia O'Keeffe, Allan Houser, Gustave Baumann, R. C. Gorman; actors Alan Arkin, Greer Garson, Errol Flynn, Gene Hackman, Val Kilmer, Carole

Burnett, Shirley MacLaine, Ali MacGraw, Julia Roberts; and singers John Denver, Burl Ives, Randy Travis.

Maria Benítez is one of the world's best performers in Flamenco dance. She began appearing in Santa Fe in the early 1970s and still performs here.

Classified climatically as a high desert, Santa Fe is 7,000 feet above sea level and averages about 300 days of sunshine a year. New Mexico's 10,000-foot topographical relief—from 2,840 to 13,160 feet—includes six of the world's seven life zones. It comprises 122,666 square miles and is the fifth-largest state in the country.

According to *The Santa Fe New Mexican*, Americans spend .9 percent of their income on alcoholic beverages and .3 percent of their income on reading materials. So, three times as much is spent on booze as on books.

The word *sopaipilla*, the unleavened bread served with honey and a New Mexican favorite, comes from the Arabic word *súppa* (bread dunked oil).

Petroglyphs are rock carvings. Pictographs are rock paintings.

Canyon Road, once an Indian trading trail to the Pecos Pueblo, is perhaps the oldest road in New Mexico.

New Mexico is the only state in the Union that has "U.S.A." on its license plates. This is to let everyone know we are one of the Fifty States.

The Conestoga covered freight wagon was so named because it was made in Conestoga, Pennsylvania.

During the Mexican occupation, Mexican women wore short full skirts and low cut blouses with shawls—the opposite of their American counterparts.

Though illegal, gambling was considered the "national sport of Mexico."

The Penitentes, a lay brotherhood that filled in for Catholic parishioners in the absence or lack of priests in New Mexico, still exist today.

Chile con carne is chile with lean pork cut into one-inch squares and boiled with sage, garlic and salt. Chile powder and flour is then added. It was one of the staples of people traveling the Santa Fe Trail.

Right: The Indian Market celebrated its 90th year in 2011. It stands as the premier cultural event in the city.

APPENDIX
(A SURVIVORS' GUIDE)

MAJOR YEARLY EVENTS AND CELEBRATIONS

Here is a list of some events you may wish to attend while in Santa Fe. You will find more in the local papers when you arrive. See the previous pages for the calendar of major Indian events. To aid in planning, you can log on to the Santa Fe Convention and Visitors Bureau Web site, which has a detailed calendar for every month of the year, with descriptions of each event and links to their Web sites.

- santafe.org/Calendar

Super Bowl Weekend

"Souper Bowl"

Fundraiser for the Food Depot where you can sample soups from the best of Santa Fe restaurants (check local newspapers for details).

Good Friday

Pilgrimage to the Santuario de Chimayó

- evanderputten.org/special/newmexico/chimayo.htm

First Tuesday in May

The Taste of Santa Fe

Sample the best dishes from the best Santa Fe restaurants. Proceeds benefit the Palace of the Governors.

Summer Music

The Santa Fe Chamber Music Festival, The Santa Fe Opera and the Santa Fe Desert Chorale all perform during the summer months.

Early June

El Rancho de Las Golondrinas Spring Festival and Annual Fair

- (505) 471-226i
- golondrinas.org

Mid-June

Buckaroo Ball

Dinner, garden tours, brunch over a three-day period, charity event
- (505) 992-3700
- buckarooball.com

Mid- to Late-June

Rodeo de Santa Fe

- 3237 Rodeo Road (at Richards Avenue and Avenida Pueblos)
- (505) 471-4300
- $7 per person matinee, $8 evening ($1 less for kids and seniors)
- rodeodesantafe.org

Late June

Taos Solar Music Festival

Eclectic music combined with solar-energy information booths and handicrafts.
- solarmusicfest.com

July

Fourth of July Pancake Breakfast

Kiwanis Club Pancake Breakfast on the Plaza

Mid-July

International Folk Art Market

Although a relatively new event, this has become the world's largest Folk Art Fair. Call for dates and directions.
- Milner Plaza on Museum Hill
- (877) 567-7380 or (505) 476-1166
- folkartmarket.org

Mid-July

El Rancho de Las Golondrinas Wine Festival

- (505) 471-2261, call for dates and directions
- golondrinas.org/julyevents.htm

Last weekend in July

Spanish Market

Oldest and largest exhibition and sale of traditional Spanish Colonial artforms in the United States.
- spanishmarket.org

Late July

Eight Northern Indian Pueblos Council Artists & Craftsmen Show

- For details on this year's show, call (505) 747-1593 Extension 112.
- eightnorthernpueblos.com

Late July

Behind Adobe Walls ®

Garden tours sponsored by the Santa Fe Garden Club.
- (505) 982-0807 or (800) 732-6881

Last Two Weeks in July

New Mexico Jazz Festival

Features local as well as world renowned artists and jazz masters and brings together the two major New Mexico cities—Albuquerque and Santa Fe in various venues in both cities.
- newmexicojazzfestival.org

Mid-August

El Rancho de Las Golondrinas

Lavender Fest with products, plants and demonstrations.
- golondrinas.org/calendar.htm

Mid- to Late-August

Santa Fe Bluegrass & Old-Time Music Festival

- southwestpickers.org/festivals.html

Weekend following the third Thursday in August

SWAIA Santa Fe Indian Market

Probably the most well known of all Santa Fe events. Over 1,000 Indian artists from across the country show their work in this famous Indian show on the Santa Fe Plaza.
- swaia.org/indianmrkt.html

Late-August

Thirsty Ear Music Festival

A festival of blues, folk, alt-country and roots-rock artists.
- thirstyearfestival.com

Early September, weekend after Labor Day

Fiestas de Santa Fe

A four-day event beginning with the burning of the three-story puppet figure Zozobra, or "Old Man Gloom." Festivities are continued on the Plaza and include the Pet Parade and the Historical/Hysterical Parade. Mass and the Processional to the Cross of the Martyrs conclude the Fiesta.

- (505) 988-7575
- santafefiesta.org
- zozobra.com

Late September

Santa Fe Wine & Chile Fiesta

- santafewineandchile.org

First Weekend in October

El Rancho de Las Golondrinas Harvest Festival

- golondrinas.org/octevents.htm

Early December

Santa Fe Film Festival

- santafefilmfestival.com

First Weekend in December

Winter Spanish Market

- spanishmarket.org

Second Friday in December

Christmas at the Palace

Open house Friday evening at the Palace of the Governors
- palaceofthegovernors.org

Third Sunday in December

Las Posadas Procession

In and around Santa Fe Plaza. Here, actors portraying Mary and

Joseph try to find an inn for the night. An actor portraying the devil hovers on the rooftops overlooking the Plaza, making sure they will have no place to rest. Eventually, they're taken in at the Palace of the Governors. This performance is a must-see!

Christmas Eve

Canyon Road Walk

This informal walk seems to be taken by all of Santa Fe and is a delight. Homes and businesses on Canyon Road put up *farolitos* (paper bags weighted with sand with candle inserted) to light your way. Bonfires (*luminaries*) and music warm the body and soul.

- santafe.com/travel/christmas.html
- santafe.com/travel/kids.html

Christmas Day

Dances at most pueblos.

Parading La Conquistadora during Fiesta, the oldest fiesta in the country.

WORDS AND PHRASES YOU'LL HEAR ABOUT TOWN

Acequia Madre - Mother Ditch. The word acequia is an old Arabic word adopted by the Spanish, meaning "canal." In New Mexico, these little canals are referred to as "ditches." Madre is the Spanish word for "mother"—hence, "Mother Ditch."

Anglo - any person not of Hispanic or Native American descent

Arroyo - a natural watercourse, usually dry (except after rainstorms)

Bajada - descent of a hill

Bulto - a statue, usually of a saint, made of carved cottonwood root

Calle - street

Canale - drain spout extending out from a parapet of a flat roof

Corbel - scroll-shaped wood bracket used to support a *viga*

Entrada - expedition or entryway

Gringo - an American, a foreigner, a "white man." One suggestion as to its origin goes that during the Mexican-American Wars, a popular song in the United States was *Green Grow the Lilacs*. American soldiers sang it, and the Mexicans took the first two words, which sounded like *gringo* to them, and gave that name to the American soldiers.

Horno - outdoor oven

Latilla - branches used for ceilings and coyote fences

Parroquia - the parish church

Portal - a long covered porch supported by corbels on posts

Posada - inn

Retablo - a wooden panel painted with a religious image for use in churches

Ristra - a string of chiles

Santero - a carver of the saints

Santo - carved saint

Trastero - a wooden cupboard

Viga - a debarked log used as a ceiling beam

Ristras or bunches of chile hanging from vigas.

WORDS FOUND ON RESTAURANT MENUS

Here are some Spanish words that will help you get around town, order in a restaurant and just plain make you part of Santa Fe.

Carne adovada - pork stew marinated in red chile sauce, usually rich, hot and delicious

Chile - chile pepper, can be red or green

Chile "Christmas" - This does not refer to the December holiday but is frequently used in restaurants in town. Since all restaurants prepare chile differently, it's hard to know if green or red chile is the hotter or tastier. The best bet is to tell your server to bring "Christmas," which means half-green, half-red chile. Incidentally, you can always ask for your chile on the side, if you are not sure you want chile at all.

Chile rellenos - moderately hot chiles stuffed with cheese then dipped in egg batter and fried

Fajitas - a very tasty combination of stir-fried onions, green peppers, and chiles plus marinated steak, chicken or shrimp, served with warm flour tortillas and condiments

Frijoles - beans

Piñon - the nut of the piñon tree, used in many dishes and salads

Sopaipillas - a classic New Mexican puffy flatbread that is deep fried and usually served with honey

Tortilla - a round fried thin flatbread made of flour or ground yellow or blue corn meal

GENERAL INFORMATION REGARDING ALBUQUERQUE, SANTA FE AND TAOS

When going by air, most travelers fly into Albuquerque, then take the one-hour shuttle trip up to Santa Fe. Driving up to Taos from Santa Fe takes about an hour and a half.

AIRLINE INFORMATION

All major U.S. airlines fly into the Albuquerque International Sunport. You can rent a car at the Sunport, or, you may take a shuttle to Santa Fe (advance reservations are recommended). The distance to Santa Fe from Albuquerque is about 62 miles, and the drive takes about an hour. Here are some numbers you may wish to keep on hand:

- Airline Reservations & Flight Information
  (505) 244-7733 (or call individual airline)

You can get detailed flight information from your airline's Web site or from the following:

- cabq.gov/airport (Albuquerque International Sunport)
- Airport Police Office
  (505) 244-7700
- Lost and Found/Paging/Skycap Assistance/Airport Parking Information (or call individual airline)

SHUTTLES TO AND FROM SANTA FE

- Roadrunner Shuttle and Charter Service
  (505) 424-3387 or (505) 424-4828
- Sandia Shuttle Express
  (888) 775-5696 or (505) 474-5696
  sandiashuttle.com
  Taos Express
  575-751-4459
  Taosexpress.com

SANTA FE MUNICIPAL AIRPORT

Santa Fe's municipal airport is located at the southwest corner of the city and handles all types of private aircraft. Check at last minute to see if any other major airlines will be shuttling into Santa Fe. Currently, American Airlines flies to Santa Fe and returns twice a day.

- Santa Fe Municipal Airport
  (505) 271-2525 (airport information line)
  airnav.com/airport/SAF
  nmohwy.com/s/saf.htm
  ohwy.com/nm/s/saf.htm
  (on-line Highways—Santa Fe Municipal Airport)
- Santa Fe Air Center (FBO)
  Charter Service
  (505) 471-2525
  santafejet.biz

AMTRAK

Albuquerque and Santa Fe (Lamy station) are served by Amtrak. Amtrak's Southwest Chief trains—eastbound from Los Angeles and westbound from Chicago—meet each afternoon at Lamy, New Mexico.

Call the Lamy Shuttle at (505) 982-8829 to make a reservation for transportation to Santa Fe (14 miles, about 20 minutes' drive time), or, notify your hotel for pickup.

- Amtrak Information and Reservations
  Local station in Lamy: (505) 466-4511
  Nationwide reservations: (800) 872-7245 or 800-USA-RAIL
  amtrak.com

SANTA FE TRAILS BUS SYSTEM

Accessible buses and bus stops are available to 50 percent of the city.
- 505-955-2001
- santafetrails.santafenm.gov

TAXIS

- Capitol City Cabs (You must call for a cab in Santa Fe)
  (505) 438-0000

SANTA FE'S WEATHER & WHAT TO WEAR

At 7,000 feet above sea level, Santa Fe is a high desert country dotted with piñon and ponderosa pines, as opposed to the giant saguaro and other cacti of lower desert elevations. We're close to the clouds and close to the sun, and our 300 days of sunshine per year are accompanied by very low humidity. This makes for warm days (rarely more than the mid-90s during June, July and August) and cool, "good sleeping" nights.

Dress in Santa Fe is casual, and shorts are fine for most summer days. The temperature drops soon after sunset, so bring a sweater or jacket along with you. Should you attend the beautiful Santa Fe Opera or other outdoor evening event, you may need a blanket or warm jacket. (We once sat next to a couple from Phoenix wearing short-sleeved shirts and wound up sharing our blanket with them.) Rain showers are short but sudden, and it is wise to check the local forecast before attending outdoor concerts.

The dress code here is relaxed, so leave your tie at home. Many locals wear a Santa Fe tuxedo when they go out on the town. What is a Santa Fe tuxedo, you ask? Well, it consists of a cowboy shirt with a bolo instead of a tie, jeans, a handcrafted leather belt with a silver buckle, cowboy boots, a cowboy hat and a sport jacket. And that's really dressing up!

Warmth often lingers into early November. After that, layer your clothes; even in winter the daytime temperatures are much warmer than those after sundown. A warm ski jacket is perfect for snowy days. We have 40-degree swings in temperature within a 24-hour period. In the winter, you may wake up to 15-degree mornings, and by 1:00 in the afternoon the temperature could be up around 45 degrees!

Average Weather Statistics
- Average Temperature
  - January: High 42-Low 19
  - July: High 86-Low 57
- Average Rainfall: 12-14 inches
- Average Snowfall: 17.5 inches

For more information, check out the Weather Channel's Web page for Santa Fe: weather.com (then input Santa Fe, NM).

STATE SYMBOLS

THE STATE FLAG OF NEW MEXICO

New Mexico's current flag is one of many to have flown over the state. It was preceded by the flags of Spain, Mexico, the Confederate States of America, the United States and an earlier state flag. That first state flag featured a small American flag in the upper left quadrant, a state seal in the lower right and the words "New Mexico" stitched diagonally in red across a dark blue background. This flag flew from 1912 to 1925, when it was replaced by the current flag, which features the red sun symbol called a "Zia" (the sun symbol of the Zia Pueblo Indians) on a field of gold. Red and gold were the colors of Queen Isabella de Castile and represented the colors of old Spain.

- 50states.com/flag/nmflag.htm
- en.wikipedia.org/wiki/New_Mexico#State_symbols

THE ZIA SUN SYMBOL

New Mexico's distinctive Zia sun symbol is closely associated with the state, whose motto is the Land of Enchantment. Inspired by a design found on a 19th-century water jar from Zia Pueblo, the symbol is made up of a circular sun with linear rays extending in four directions. To the Zia people, four is a significant number. It incorporates the four directions of the Earth and the four seasons of the year, along with the four times of the day—sunrise, noon, evening and night. It also represents life's four divisions—childhood,

The State Flag of New Mexico flies below the American flag.

youth, adulthood and old age. The symbol states that everything is bound together in a circle of life, without beginning and without end. The Zia believe that in this Great Brotherhood of all things, man has four sacred obligations to maintain—a strong body, a clear mind, a pure spirit and a devotion to the welfare of his people.

- nmsu.edu/-bho/zia.html

OTHER OFFICIAL STATE SYMBOLS

State Amphibian

The 2003 state Legislature chose the New Mexico spadefoot toad (*Spea multiplicata*) as the official state amphibian. This medium-sized desert-dwelling toad is greenish, gray or brown, with scattered darker spots or blotches. Its eyes show vertical pupils in bright light. Each hind foot features a wedge-shaped spade, which enables it to burrow deep into the ground. These toads are most easily seen and heard after a summer rain. They are found statewide.

- en.wikipedia.org/wiki/Spea_multiplicata

State Animal

The black bear (*Ursus americanus*) is common in wooded areas throughout New Mexico. Smokey, probably the most famous bear in the history of the United States, was a New Mexico cub found cowering in a tree after a forest fire in the Lincoln National Forest near Capitan.

- en.wikipedia.org/wiki/American_Black_Bear
- smokeybear.com/vault/default.asp

State Bird

The friendly roadrunner (*Geococcyx californianus*), a type of cuckoo, can run at speeds of up to 20 mph! Adult birds are as large as two feet long, half of that being tail. The birds rarely fly and do not migrate.

- 50states.com/bird/roadrunn.htm

State Butterfly

The Sandia hairstreak (*Callophrys* [Sandia] *mcfarlandi*), a small

green-and-gold butterfly found in much of the state, was chosen the state
butterfly in 2003.
- butterfliesandmoths.org/species?l=1527
- nearctica.com/butter/plate8/Cmcfar.htm

State Cookie

In 1989 the bizcochito (bees-ko-CHEE-toh) was named the state cookie. New Mexico is the first state to have an official state cookie and probably the only one to use the traditional lard instead of butter as a chief
cookie ingredient.
- shgresources.com/nm/symbols/cookie/
- en.wikibooks.org/wiki/Cookbook:Bizcochito

State Fish

The Rio Grande cutthroat trout (*Onchorhynchus clarki virgina-
lis*) is native to the mountain streams and lakes of Northern New
Mexico.
- westerntrout.org/trout/profiles/rgct.html
- sangres.com/sports/fish/fishingnm.htm

State Flower

The yucca (*Yucca glauca*), called "Our Lord's Candles" by early settlers
who admired the beautiful flowers of this cactus, is abundant throughout
New Mexico.
- en.wikipedia.org/wiki/Yucca
- netstate.com/states/symb/flowers/nm_yucca_flower.htm

State Fossil

The Coelophysis (SEE-low-FIE-sis), an ancient, meat-eating creature,
is New Mexico's only Triassic-era dinosaur. Originally discovered in Rio
Arriba County, this dinosaur was deemed the state fossil in 1987. Coelophysis (which means "hollow form") was a small, lightweight dinosaur
that walked on two long legs and had light, hollow bones.
- en.wikipedia.org/wiki/Coelophysis

State Gem

Turquoise (hydrated copper aluminum phosphate), a gemstone favored by the Indians long before the Spanish arrived, is the most popular gem of jewelers and silversmiths in New Mexico.
- en.wikipedia.org/wiki/Turquoise
- jewelry.about.com/library/weekly/aa062902a.htm

State Grass

The blue gramma (*Bouteloua gracilis*) is found all over the state, especially on grasslands and bottomlands between altitudes of 3,000 and 8,000 feet. It thrives in dry climates.
- turf.uiuc.edu/turfSpecies/Boutelouagracilis.html

State Insect

The tarantula hawk wasp (*Pepsis formosa*) was selected as the state insect by elementary-school vote in 1989. It is found in New Mexico and other Southwestern states.
- desertusa.com/mag01/sep/papr/thawk.html

State Question

In 1998 the New Mexico State legislature passed a House Joint Memorial declaring "Red or Green" as the official state question. This refers to the question always asked whether one prefers red or green chile when ordering New Mexico cuisine. With adoption of the state question New Mexico is acknowledging the financial gain and national recognition that chile generates for the state.
- en.wikipedia.org/wiki/New_Mexico#State_symbols

State Reptile

The New Mexico whiptail lizard became the official state reptile in 2003. All these little striped lizards are female—they actually reproduce by cloning themselves!
- en.wikipedia.org/wiki/Cnemidophorus_neomexicanus

State Slogan

Adopted by the Legislature in 1975, "Everybody is somebody in New Mexico" is the official state slogan for business, commerce and industry in New Mexico.

State Tree

The piñon pine (*Pinus edulis*), a sturdy, slow-growing little evergreen, flourishes over vast areas of the state. The piñon produces tiny, tasty nuts that are highly prized by gourmet cooks, and the pleasant, distinctive scent of burning logs perfumes New Mexico's air in cold weather.

- en.wikipedia.org/wiki/Pinyon_pine

State Vegetables

Chiles and *frijoles*! Chile, often teamed up with pinto beans, is a unique element of the New Mexico diet. Chile plants were brought by the Spanish settlers to New Mexico from Mexico, where the Aztecs had cultivated the plants for centuries. Chile is the New Mexico state vegetable even though it is technically a fruit. The word "chile" refers to the pepper; the spelling "chili" refers to chile combined with other ingredients such as beans. Many people, especially those not from the Southwest, mistakenly spell chile as chili.

- www-psych.nmsu.edu/~linda/chile.htm
- en.wikipedia.org/wiki/Chili_pepper

Pinto beans have been a staple of the Pueblo Indians' diet since prehistoric times. An excellent source of protein, the medium-sized pinto bean (*frijole*) is a hybrid that takes its name from the Spanish word for "painted." Light brown, with dark-brown spatter markings, pintos fade to a uniform dull brown color after cooking.

- co.essortment.com/drypintobeans_rjtr.htm

For more information on state symbols:

- netstate.com/states/symb/nm_symb.htm

Zozobra

Santa Fe artist Will Shuster (1893-1969) drew heavily upon local customs and ceremonies as subjects for his art, so it seems only fitting that he played a part in creating one of Santa Fe's most popular rituals. Perhaps the most well-loved and well-known Shuster creation is Zozobra, the forty-nine-foot paper puppet, also known as Old Man Gloom, whose annual burning signifies the exoneration of last year's sorrows and the beginning of the Santa Fe Fiesta. Originally created by Shuster in 1926, Zozobra has become a Santa Fe legend.

- zozobra.com
- zozobra.com/history.html

USEFUL WEBSITES

Some links with useful information for Albuquerque, Santa Fe and Taos. These are subject to change.

- Santa Fe Convention and Visitors Bureau

    santafe.org

- New Mexico Department of Tourism, statewide attractions and maps

    newmexico.org

- CultureNetWork, an on-line directory of artists, artisans, arts organizations, galleries and others involved in the cultural life of New Mexico

    nmculturenet.org

- *Santa Fe On Line Magazine*, listings and reviews of accommodations and restaurants with addresses and phone numbers, also attractions and the arts

    santafe.com

- official website of the city of Santa Fe

    sfweb.ci.santa-fe.nm.us

- locally-oriented city guide continuously updated by residents, also useful for visitors who want to experience the local flavor

    santafeusa.us/

- Santa Fe Chamber of Commerce

    santafechamber.com

- website for the *Santa Fean* magazine, contains features relating specifically to Santa Fe, especially art and culture, also selected local links

    santafean.com

- *New Mexico Magazine*, statewide attractions and features, also Internet links sorted by category, including hundreds for Santa Fe alone

  nmmagazine.com
- Taos Chamber of Commerce

  taoschamber.com/
- Ski New Mexico

  skinewmexico.com
- a comprehensive guide to Santa Fe for travelers, locals and merchants

  santafe.nm-unlimited.net
- New Mexico Office of Cultural Affairs

  nmoca.org
- New Mexico's Cultural Treasures database

  nmculture.org
- directory of Santa Fe commercial websites

  santafe.net
- another directory of Santa Fe commercial websites

  santafestation.com
- another directory of Santa Fe commercial websites, includes Albuquerque

  santafeez.com

About the Author and Photographer

JOEL B. STEIN is a tour guide for the Palace of the Governors and a professional tour guide as well, giving tours of historic downtown Santa Fe. Additionally, he conducts tours in Bandelier National Monument, Taos and other out-of-town venues. Stein has done independent research about Santa Fe and is a collector of Indian cultural objects and American folk art. He and his wife, Mary, are actively involved in the Santa Fe community.

ALAN PEARLMAN has photographed extensively throughout the Southwest. His photographs have been shown in several one-person and group exhibitions, including *Through the Lens: Creating Santa Fe at Santa Fe's Palace of the Governors* in 2009. He lives in Santa Fe with his wife, Gail Bass, a musician and jewelry maker.

Acknowledgements

Research plays a major role in assembling information for a travel book. I have many individuals and organizations to thank for their kind help and support. My thanks to Mary Stein, my wife and soul mate, who became my "editor extraordinaire"; all the docents of the Palace of the Governors for their camaraderie, good spirit and love of history; Mary G. Clark, whose late husband, Edward, started a guidebook years ago and is quoted in this book; Kyle Grey of the Santa Fe Opera; Julie Adams of the Santa Fe Chamber Music Festival; Will Channing, who sold us one of our first Indian artifacts many years ago and helped send us on our way to Santa Fe; the *Visitors Guide* of the Eight Northern Indian Pueblos; the New Mexico Department of Tourism; Andrew Neighbour, who designed a memorable cover and logo; Mary Neighbour who did the interior graphic design and helped to guide me through the intricate maze of publishing; Kay Carlson, who put up with me during the word processing phase; and my legal beagle, Lee Warren.

Source Notes

Chávez, Thomas E. *New Mexico Past and Present*. University of New Mexico Press, 2006.

Clark, Edward C. *Chimayó*. Unpublished manuscript, Santa Fe, 1995.

Cline, Lynn. *Literary Pilgrims, The Santa Fe & Taos Writers Colonies 1917-1950*, University of New Mexico Press, 2007.

Cline, Mary Kay. Albuquerque, *Portrait of a Western City*, Clear Light Publishing, 2006.

Cook, Mary Jean and Cordelia Snow. *Palace Walking Tour Historic Events*. Docent brochure, Palace of the Governors, Santa Fe, 1997.

Grant, D.N. *Santa Fe: History of Our Ancient City*. Santa Fe: School of American Research Press, 1989 and 2008.

Jung, C.G. *Memories, Dreams, Reflections*. Aniela Jaffé, editor. Richard and Clara Winston, translators. New York: Vintage Books (a division of Random House), 1989.

La Farge, John Pen. *Turn Left at the Sleeping Dog*. Albuquerque: University of New Mexico Press, 2001.

Lawrence, D.H. *Essay*, N.p., c. 1924.

Palace of the Governors Lectures. Docent lecture series, Palace of the Governors, Santa Fe, 1999.

Poling-Kempes, Lesley. *Valley of the Shining Stone: The Story of Abiquiú*. Tucson: University of Arizona Press, 1997.

Simmons, Mark. Column, *Santa Fe New Mexican*, April 27, 2002.

Terrell, John Upton. *Pueblos Gods and Spaniards*. Dial Press, 1973.

Uhlenhopp, Jack. *Docent Notes on the Palace of the Governors*. Oral transmission, Santa Fe, June 2002.

Index

Numerals

Page numbers in bold indicate illustrations.

Vista Clara Ranch Resort and Spa
125
Vollertsen, John 86

W

Walatowa village 169
walking and custom tours 28–35
walking tour of old Santa Fe 12–27
Wallace, General Lew 9, 185
Washington, D.C. 131
Waters, Frank 10
Water Street area 20–22
Watts, Alan 154
Weather Channel 197
weather in Santa Fe 197–198
weaving 9, 62, 132, 144, 146–147, 171
West, Bill 142
Westwind Travel 34
Wheeler Peak 150
Wheelwright, Mary Cabot 59
Wheelwright Museum of the
American Indian 59, 112
whiptail lizard 201
White, Amelia 55
Wild Hogs 8, 44
wildlife 140
wine festival 62, 189
wineries 134
Wine Spectator 68
Wine Spectator Award of Excellence
82
Wingswest Birding Tours 142
Winter Spanish Market 191
winter sports 142–143

Witch Ranch 127
Wolashuk, Nicolas 100
woodcarving 148

Y

yucca 200
Yucca glauca 200

Z

Zaplin-Lampert Gallery 101
Zia bird symbol 171
Zia Diner 85
Zia Pueblo 24, 171, 176, 179, 198
Zia Cultural Center 171
Zia sun symbol 198
zozobra 4
Zozobra 4, 191, 202
Zuckerman, Pinchas 39
Zuni language 159
Zuni Pueblo 172–173, 178–180